THE RESCUE

ANDY McNAB

THE RESCUE

**The True Story of the SAS Mission to
Save Hostages from the Taliban**

WELBECK

Published in 2023 by Welbeck
An imprint of Welbeck Non-Fiction Limited
Part of the Welbeck Publishing Group
Offices in: London – 20 Mortimer Street, London W1T 3JW &
Sydney – 205 Commonwealth Street, Surry Hills 2010, NSW, Australia
www.welbeckpublishing.com

A CIP catalogue record for this book is available from the British Library.

ISBNs
Hardback – 9781802796858
Trade Paperback – 9781802796865
eBook – 9781802796872

Typeset by seagulls.net
AUS/NZ edition printed and bound in Australia by the Opus Group
All other editions printed and bound in the UK

10 9 8 7 6 5 4 3 2 1

AUTHOR'S NOTE

Beginning with my previous title, *The Hunt*, in 2022 I launched a new series of books that chronicle special forces missions around the world. The aim of this series is to inform and pay homage to the people involved in these difficult and dangerous operations. Many of these raids are still secret, and the existing details on the missions are scarce, but there is rarely a day that goes by where elite soldiers are not planning for, or executing, a dangerous mission. From the dusty streets of Basra to the dense jungles of South America, the world's most dedicated soldiers hunt down their enemies with ruthless intent.

The Hunt was one such story, but not all special forces missions are to kill or capture. Some are to gather intelligence, while others are launched in order to rescue innocent victims who have been kidnapped. The book you are holding in your hands, *The Rescue*, is the story of one of these missions.

In order to protect those involved, and those still serving, names and tactics have been changed so that nothing of use is handed over to the enemy. *The Rescue* is based on fact, and you won't read anything in this book that hasn't occurred in real life. The characters are based on real people; sometimes they are an amalgam of different characters I've come into contact with and sometimes precise portraits of exact people, but with identifying characteristics changed. Other characters are representative of the nature of their trade. For instance, in this book, Wazir is an Afghan intelligence asset. His part in *The Rescue* is representative of this real-life role that local forces make in support of British missions in Afghanistan.

Though the special forces are the ones at the tip of the spear, a successful rescue is not possible without intelligence analysts, aircrews and other supporting roles. *The Rescue* widens the cast of characters beyond the SAS and US Navy SEALs in order to reflect this reality.

For those who are unfamiliar with SEAL Team Six – also known as DEVGRU (Development Group) – they are one of the world's most elite units, and have fought side by side with the SAS and SBS on many occasions. There is a high degree of respect between these operators who have fought and bled for each other. The war in Afghanistan was a multinational effort, and nowhere was this cooperation closer than with the special forces, including the Afghan republic's own commando units.

This story is a testament to the skill, bravery and selflessness of those who would place the lives of others above their own. No matter the place, no matter the risks, no matter the danger, the SAS and DEVGRU continue to cement their reputation among the best of the best.

Andy McNab

CHAPTER 1

KUNAR PROVINCE, AFGHANISTAN, OCTOBER 2010

The moon was full as they flew into the 'Valley of Death'. It was American soldiers who had given the Korengal its nickname, and they had good reason to do so: the steep, wooded mountains made patrolling, holding and resupplying the area especially perilous. This valley had been the site of some of the most brutal fighting of the war, with outposts almost overrun by the swarming enemy. In the end, the US Army had decided that staying here was too costly. They committed increasing numbers of troops to other parts of Afghanistan, but the Korengal had been abandoned to the Taliban, with the last US forces pulling out of the deadly valley in April.

But tonight they were coming back.

Accompanied by a pair of Apache attack helicopters riding shotgun, two CH-47 Chinooks flew high in the moonlight, their twin rotors beating in a thudding rhythm that was familiar to friendly forces and enemy alike. The Chinooks belonged to the 160th Special Operations Aviation Regiment (SOAR), and were operated by the US Army's top aviators, crew chiefs, and support staff. Almost everyone on board would have agreed with that. They were American, after all, but not Sergeant Harry Allen. Born in Stirling, Scotland, Allen had worked with them across the world on operations. This wasn't his first trip to a war zone, and Allen had hundreds of missions under his belt. In his 14 years of service, seven of them in the Special Air Service (SAS), the tall, intense man had forgotten more about soldiering than most people would ever know about it.

Thirty-five years old, but with a thick black beard and sun-darkened skin that made him look older than he was, Allen wasn't put off by the Korengal's nickname. He hadn't joined the SAS looking for a picnic. He was here for a fight, and the Valley of Death sounded like the place to find it. In 2008, nearly three-quarters of the bombs dropped by NATO had fallen on and around these mountains, which spoke of the intensity of the combat that had taken place here. Unlike other parts of the country, in the Korengal the Americans hadn't found willing partners among the locals. Maybe things could have turned out differently. Incidents like the shooting of a cow by US soldiers, and their refusal to pay compensation, had certainly cemented local opinion. In their eyes, the Americans were invaders, just like the Soviet soldiers who had come here in the eighties. They had been driven out, too. The bones of some Soviets still lay scattered on the mountainsides. With harsh winters and an equally harsh population, the Korengal wasn't a place that took prisoners.

The only time that Allen had ever felt like he'd been a prisoner was back in school. It wasn't that he didn't have the aptitude for education; far from it. He'd just felt frustrated – held back by those who didn't want to excel, like he did. This carried over into every part of his life. He was the first to get on the case of a teammate who was slacking on the sports field, and that attitude persisted when he joined the army. When Allen had arrived as an 18-year-old at his infantry regiment, he'd been disappointed. He'd assumed that everyone would be as keen as him. Instead, some of his fellow soldiers did the bare minimum, and sometimes less than that. A few were alcoholics. Others were overweight, and failed fitness tests. Allen just couldn't understand that mentality. Why would someone join the military and not give it their all? Where was their sense of pride? Where was their professionalism?

Enough was enough. The first chance that he got, and with a couple of the more driven men in his regiment, Allen had attempted special forces selection. He was one of the youngest men to arrive at the training wing in Stirling Lines, Hereford, and no one had expected him to pass. No one except himself. By the time the gruelling selection process was over, Allen was one of the few men left standing, and he was 'badged', awarded his sand-coloured beret, marking him as a member of the SAS. Since then he had performed long-range patrols and recces in bandit country, guarded British VIPs, and kicked in doors in Iraq and Afghanistan. Before his latest posting he had been the troop sergeant of one of the elite regiment's Air Troops, the regiment's free-fall specialists, and loved every second. Allen enjoyed parachuting as much as he did going on raids and recces, and everything else that the regiment had thrown at him.

Tonight, he was part of a Deliberate Option, the Brits' term for a planned and coordinated attack to rescue a hostage.

Allen and the rest of the team knew everyone of importance that could have an effect on the plan. Be it the enemy or the hostage, it was an important part of the briefing process. The team studied photographs – taken from intelligence sources, or even social media pages – until the faces were seared into their memories. When instant decisions needed to be made, there wasn't time to second-guess. Was that man an innocent bystander or were they throwing their hands up seeking to cause confusion so that they could lure soldiers within suicide vest range? Faces mattered. So did age, build, colour, distinguishing marks, height, face, gait and hair. Kidnappers can swap clothes with their hostages in the confusion of a chaotic gunfight in an attempt to escape. Weird things happened in the battlespace, be that in the mountains of Afghanistan or the streets of its cities, and it was the small details that allowed Allen to decide whom to kill and whom to rescue.

The Scotsman lived and breathed soldiering. He trained hard with his squadron, and in his own time he pushed himself physically, and read about wars, and how to win them. Allen wasn't interested in the pub. He'd grown up with a dad who'd prioritised booze over his own children, and Allen wouldn't choose hangovers over his career. He was only interested in being the best, just like the recruiting adverts had offered back when he was a kid. He'd come a long way since then.

Despite the danger that they were heading into – and more likely, because of it – Allen smiled to himself. The sound of the Chinook's beating rotors was an ever-present sound that stifled all but shouted conversation. In the darkness a man was left with his thoughts, and in his a memory came back to Allen. He'd been a recruit when the cavalry officer had made his men learn the poem 'The Charge of the

Light Brigade' by Alfred, Lord Tennyson, and a few of the lines returned to him now.

Theirs not to reason why,
Theirs but to do and die:
Into the valley of Death
Rode the six hundred.

Allen agreed with the first two lines – he didn't question why he was at war, he just gave it everything he had – but there wouldn't be 600 riding into the Valley of Death tonight. Little more than 50 men were heading into the Korengal. Twenty of them were from the elite US Navy SEAL Team Six, which had been founded by legendary SEAL Richard 'Dick' Marcinko and carried out similar roles to the SAS and SBS. There were some 2,400 active-duty SEALs, but fewer than 10 per cent of them served in Team Six, known as the Development Group, or DEVGRU, by those in the job. A SEAL could pass the demanding challenge of the Basic Underwater Demolition Training and its famous 'Hell Week', but DEVGRU had its own entry process that was more akin to the special forces selection of Britain's SAS and SBS. The Brits and Americans cross-trained often, and since the Global War on Terror had begun in 2001, they were often fighting side by side. The SEALs sent men to learn from the Brits, and the SAS and SBS sent men to learn from the Americans. Allen was on an 18-month embed to watch, learn, advise and, on special occasions, join the action.

Tonight was one of the latter. A British hostage, who had been in the country as an aid worker, was being held in the

5

Korengal, and her time was running out. Usually a nation like Britain, with elite units trained in hostage rescue, would go after their own people, but the SEALs were in the right place at the right time. They knew Kunar as well as any unit, and America had offered their help to rescue the British hostage. The US was Britain's closest ally, and it was critical that a rescue be launched immediately.

'Local elders have been encouraging the Taliban to kill her,' the intelligence officer had told them in the briefing. 'They're saying that they should do the same thing to her as they did to the Russian. No doubt a Soviet soldier had fallen into their hands during the last war. However he died, it wouldn't have been quick. Before Al-Qaeda became famous for it, the mujahideen of Afghanistan were filming their executions, cutting the throats of prisoners, or pulling them apart limb by limb with horses.'

Places like the Korengal weren't just valleys of death. They were valleys of horror. There were no guarantees in war, but on this mission Allen was certain of two things: any mistake could be fatal, and falling into enemy hands was a fate worse than death.

Allen looked around at the cramped confines of the Chinook. He wondered what was going through the minds of the SEALs around him. Close to the border to Pakistan, the northeast of the country had been the site of Operation Red Wings, where a SEAL reconnaissance mission had been compromised and attacked, leaving only one of them alive. And then, during the rescue mission, a Chinook, call sign Extortion 17, had been hit by a rocket-propelled grenade (RPG). The RPG had been fired when the heli was hovering so that the SEALs could fast-rope to the ground. It was a devastating hit, and losses were catastrophic. All 38 people on board Extortion 17 were killed, 17 of them SEALs. It was the biggest single-mission loss of life in Naval Special Warfare history, and Allen was in no doubt that the experienced operators around him would have known, and been friends with, those who died that day. He didn't worry that it would affect this mission though, not in the least. From everything that he'd seen since he'd embedded with DEVGRU, they were as dedicated and professional as any fighting force in the world. Allen couldn't bring himself to say out loud that they were as good as the SAS, but with his own eyes he saw the truth. Both units were cut from the same cloth, and the most skilled warriors on the planet. The only thing that Allen would give the Americans the win on was patriotism. Their base had more flags than Buckingham Palace.

As well as the Chinook full of SEALs, 24 US Army Rangers were also inbound to the target on the second heli. These men had gone through their own arduous selection process to earn their place on the battlefield. They were fit, well-trained and highly motivated soldiers. Much like the Parachute Regiment does for the SAS, the Rangers provide a high number of candidates for US Army Special Forces selection, and some of the men flying into the Valley of Death would go on to join the Green Berets. Some might even make it to the best of the best: the Combat Applications Group (CAG), better known as Delta Force. Tonight, the Rangers would provide a security cordon while the SEALs hit the compound where the hostage was being held, and would need to fight off any Taliban attempts to reinforce the kidnappers. Given the history of the valley, it seemed impossible that the enemy would let the Americans come in without a fight.

Suddenly, Allen felt his stomach rise as the Chinook fell steeply to drop altitude. They were heading down into the mountain passes, and as the helicopter drew closer to the peaks, strong winds began to hit the bulky frame from all sides. The Chinook started to buck like an unbroken horse, the pilots using every bit of their training and skill to ride their choppers through the twists and turns of the hostile land. Looking through their night-vision goggles (NVGs), the land ahead was a sea of different shades of green. The full moon was good for the pilots' night vision, but there were two sides to every coin: the Taliban would be able to see better, too.

Allen braced himself by pushing his back against the wall and his feet into the deck. He pulled his own NVGs into place, and looked up and down the airframe, seeing the aircrew's gunners in position behind their miniguns, searching out enemy targets. If someone did open fire on the Chinook they'd be greeted by an unbroken stream of 7.62mm rounds, the miniguns firing at a rate of 2,000–6,000 rounds a minute, or up to 60 a second. Allen wouldn't want to be on the end of that.

He turned as he felt someone tapping his leg. It was the SEAL beside him, a big guy from Fort Worth, Texas, who went by the nickname Tex. Tex had won a football scholarship to the University of Texas in Austin, and Allen didn't envy the people that had played against him: the man was built like the side of a stadium.

Tex put a palm-sized tin of something into Allen's hand. 'What is it?' Allen shouted over the noise of the rotors. 'Dip!'

Allen had tried 'dip' once, and only once, back in the SEALs' base in Virginia Beach. Chewing tobacco was popular with a lot of the American military, who would place it between their lip and gum, while carrying a paper-cup. In his early days working with the SEALs, Allen thought the whole camp was addicted to coffee until someone took the lid off and gobbed into their spittoon. Claiming that it gave them energy and focus didn't really chime with Allen. It had just made him feel sick. There were plenty of British soldiers who smoked, but Allen had never been one of them. He was a straight-edged guy, and the thought of flying into combat was giving him all the focus that he needed. He handed the tin back without opening it, and heard the Texan laugh. A few seconds later the smell of tobacco hit Allen's nostrils as Tex put a huge pinch of the stuff in his mouth.

Seated on Allen's other side was Justin Miller, a wiry man from Montana. Miller had been a teenage runaway to avoid having the shit kicked out of him by his drunk stepfather, and had ended up as a ranch hand before Al-Qaeda's attacks on 9/11. The next day he was at the front of a 100-metre-long line at a recruiting office, ready to play his part in taking the war to those who had attacked America. Miller was calm and collected, and from everything that Allen had seen, an excellent assaultman.

Miller hadn't met any aid workers in-country and he didn't want to, because he didn't care for them much. They were always sticking their heads into the lion's mouth with no thought to what would happen if the lion shut its jaws. Then they expected people like him to put their lives at risk to save them. He put journalists in the same category. Where did service to a greater good end and selfish risk-taking begin? He knew of one journalist who had to be ransomed or rescued three times. On the third time, one of the assaulting special forces operators was killed. The team made the journalist carry the dead man to the helicopter, hoping it would teach him a lesson. It didn't. He was kidnapped a fourth time. Miller had no patience for a person like that.

Like most of the men on the Chinook, Allen was armed with the HK416. The 5.56mm carbine, the shorter-barrelled version of the HK416 assault rifle, making it ideal for close-quarter special operations. Manufactured by Heckler & Koch, the HK416 was based on the American M4 but was less prone to malfunction. In the close-quarter combat that SEAL Team Six usually found themselves in, any stoppage in a weapon could prove deadly. The HK416 also had a rail system which could be fitted with a variety of optics, as well as devices such as torches, laser modules and various grips. Allen was a big fan of the weapon system. Like him it wasn't flashy, but it did its job, and it did it well.

Some of the assaulters also carried Benelli shotguns, and all had SIG Sauer sidearms. Two SEAL snipers would be staying on board the Chinook, and providing more precision top cover than the door gunners and Apaches could give. The Rangers that were flying in support of DEVGRU were primarily armed with the M4 carbine, but they were also bringing along sniper rifles and light machine guns to deal with more long-range threats that might engage the rescue force. In Allen's experience, nothing settled a firefight like belt-fed weapons.

Of course the Taliban had their own weapons, and no doubt they would be dug in and positioned along the high ground of the Korengal. US military helicopters had been shot down here before. The most dangerous of the Taliban's belt-fed weapons was the 12.7mm DShK, nicknamed the Dushka. Similar to a Western .50 cal, the DShK threw out bullets the size of a man's little finger. They could shoot up engines, punch through armour and tear huge holes in human beings. Darkness and speed were the helicopter's best defence against enemy machine guns and RPGs, and flying at night was a speciality of the 160th SOAR – their nickname was 'The Night Stalkers' – but once over the target, there would be a moment where the Chinooks were sitting ducks. Allen could only hope that the Taliban hadn't sited and ranged weapons to cover the compound where the hostage was being held.

Allen didn't have access to the radio channel between the aircraft – that was the job of the joint terminal attack controllers (JTACs) – but he knew from the briefing that the Chinooks and Apaches weren't the only NATO aircraft in the sky over the Korengal that night. Predator drones had been relaying information on the target compound, and a soldier's best friend, the AC-130 Spectre gunship, would be on station to provide fire support if things got loud and angry. The AC-130 was a flying battleship: the converted C-130 Hercules carried weapons platforms that included

105mm howitzer artillery pieces, 40mm rapid-fire Bofors cannons, and 25mm or even 40mm Gatling guns. They were all online to the aircraft's sophisticated sensors, navigation and fire control systems that were able to provide surgical firepower, firing at an individual, or area saturation, attacking a convoy or large compound. The fire control system could even have different weapons attack different targets a kilometre apart at the same time. The AC-130s had a few nicknames – 'Spooky' and 'Ghostrider' were a couple – but Allen's favourite was 'The Angel of Death'. It felt good to know that such a powerful weapons platform was watching your back.

The sergeant was broken from his thoughts as a shout came from the cockpit, relayed from man to man until it reached Allen's ears.

'Two minutes!' he shouted, passing the message on to Tex.

Allen unclipped the heavy gloves from his plate carrier and pulled them on. With such wooded and uneven terrain, the quickest way onto the target was by fast-rope.

The pilot suddenly pulled the helicopter into a tight turn, pushing Allen back on the bench. In the back of the Chinook, no one was talking. A few of the more religious men were silently offering prayers, but most were thinking back to their briefing, playing through their minds the actions that would unfold in the next few minutes.

Allen lurched towards the cockpit as the pilot flared the aircraft's nose, dropping speed quickly to make as hard of a target as he could. Seconds later, the aircraft hung still in the air. On the ramp the crew tossed out thick ropes that were fixed inside the airframe. They pulled on them to test the strength, then pushed the ropes into the hands of the two closest assaultmen.

'Go!'

CHAPTER 2

One by one the SEALs took the rope and disappeared from sight. Allen shuffled forward towards the ramp. In front of him Tex took the rope and vanished. Allen put his gloved hands onto it, and dropped down to the target. It was a short, controlled fall. The pilot was one of the best in the world and had put the rear of his aircraft five metres above a roof in the target compound. Sometimes there was a danger in assaulting from the top down, as some roofs were shoddy and an operator could fall straight through them, but the Korengal was a place where heavy snow came in the winter. If the roof could take the weight of that, then it could take the weight of a man in light equipment. Even one as big as Tex.

Allen's boots hit the roof. He let go of the rope, pulling off his gloves and discarding them onto the tiles as he moved away, and brought his carbine up into the low ready position. He was the fifth man in a six-man assault team, and he followed behind Tex across the rooftop. Hot rotor wash and dust blew all around him. Allen looked left and right, taking in everything. To his left, the compound's wall was five metres tall, and beyond it Allen could see the second Chinook and the figures of Rangers fast-roping into the mountain's thick canvas of trees. To his right was a second building, towards which the second assault team was approaching after fast-roping from the aircraft's side door. The SEALs would hit both buildings at once, leaving the hostage-takers with no place to hide. Any fleeing figures would be picked up on the thermal vision by the circling Predator drones, and 'The Angel of Death'.

The men ahead of Allen came to a stop at a door on the end of the rooftop and stacked up along the wall beside it. Within seven seconds of the ropes going out of the Chinook, the men of Allen's assault team were in position. Allen felt a tap on his shoulder to let him know that the last man was in place, and he did the same to the man in front of him. The action was repeated down the line, and then a Benelli shotgun boomed twice as the Chinook put its nose down and cleared the area. Its hinges blown away, the door was blasted inwards by the strength of the rotor wash before it needed to be kicked. A second assaultman reached around the first and tossed a flash-bang grenade through the open door. Bangs and flashes of blinding light echoed from the stairwell, and then the snake of men was moving.

It was then that the Taliban opened fire. Somewhere in the compound an AK was firing on full automatic, but the sound was cut short before the Talib could empty his magazine.

'Target down,' Allen heard on his radio. He recognised the voice. It belonged to a SEAL sniper who was circling in the helicopters. SEAL stood for Sea, Air and Land, and the sniper was proof that death for the enemy could come from anywhere.

Allen kept his own weapon in the low ready. There were teammates ahead of him and he was in no immediate danger. The SEALs had been happy enough to have a Brit on the assault force, but they had trained for this moment, and sacrificed so much to be at the tip of the spear. Wild horses couldn't have pulled them from their position at the front of the stack, and Allen wouldn't have asked them to give it up. This was their rodeo.

The assault team plunged into the building and moved down the stairwell. Allen heard a carbine fire three times, and then once more. When he reached the bottom of the stairwell, he stepped across a body. There was no need to look at the dead man. The leading assaulter knew his job, and had put an extra round into the Taliban fighter's head as he'd passed him, leaving no risk for the men following behind.

The building had thick walls and rooms separated with heavy blankets that acted as curtained doors. Allen saw one jerk as rounds pushed through it, fired from the other side, but no SEAL was hit. They were keeping the thick walls between them and the next room, moving like ghosts in a seamless movement from cover to cover. The operators didn't have to think. They were America's elite, and through thousands of hours of training, and hundreds of operations, fighting in confined spaces was as instinctual to them as breathing. This enabled the operators to focus fully on what was happening about them rather than concern themselves with what their kit and weapon were doing. Everything was automatic, something that happened without thinking.

Not knowing if the hostage was on the other side of the hanging blankets, no one returned fire. Instead, Allen watched as a pair of SEALs took positions either side of the doorway. A flash-bang grenade was tossed through, the flash of the detonation lighting up the room with its 16 maroons now bursting from their casing and a strobe flashing with blinding light. The second man was already moving in, and firing. Tap-tap. Tap-tap. Double-tapped headshots to ensure they were no longer a threat in such a confined space.

Two targets down.

'Room clear! No hostage!'

Allen swore under his breath. With every second they were on the target, her chances of survival got worse. A lot worse.

'Allen, Miller,' the team leader shouted, 'Room left! Move!'

No more time to think. He was up, positioning himself on one side of the door, with Miller on the other. Allen looked at the man, about to give him the nod to kick in the door when it flew outwards, hitting Miller in the face. A young Afghan came running through the space, screaming.

'Allahu Akbar!'

Allen didn't even think about what he did next.

Dipping his head so that the maximum amount of helmet delivered the good news, he head-butted hard into the target's face. The man dropped like liquid and Allen double-tapped into his skull.

'Suicide vests!' The warning was carried over the team net. 'Miller, you okay?'

'Easy day.' The SEAL replied in the language of the teams and Allen understood that the man meant he was good to go.

'Do it,' Allen said, and Miller lobbed a flash-bang into the room. Allen followed through with his weapon in the high ready position, clearing the funnel of the doorway as Miller followed through and moved to the left. They swept their weapons over a miserable-looking room of wooden furniture and threadbare carpets. Inside reeked of body odour.

Mindful of booby traps, and with Miller covering, Allen pulled carpets away, looking for spider holes that an enemy could hide in for ambush, or tunnels that they could use to escape. They found neither.

'Room clear!' Miller shouted.

'Let's join back on the others,' Allen said.

All across the compound, pairs of assaulters were going through the methodical process. The SEALs had a saying that 'fast is smooth and smooth is fast', meaning that the best way to clear a building – and the quickest – was not to charge around like bulls but to approach it methodically. Of course, there was nothing gentle about it. Violence of Action was one of the three core principles of Close Quarters Battle, and when the SEALs found their enemies they put them down without mercy. There could be no other way. Not when a hostage's life and their own was on the line, and the enemy were wearing suicide vests.

In the distance, machine guns barked to life. 'Rangers under contact,' the team leader told them over the net.

As Allen and Miller rejoined the back of the team they heard the sound of something heavier in action. Allen reckoned it was the familiar sound of an AC-130's 25mm six-barrelled Gatling gun 'buzzing' as it fired hundreds of rounds with each four-second burst from high in the sky. The thick wooded hills didn't give the enemy protection; the aircraft's onboard technology picked out individual targets and destroyed them with industrial ease. Still, it sounded like a full-scale firefight was now in progress, and when

Allen peered through an open doorway into the compound's yard, he saw lines of red and green tracer flying across the sky at each other from multiple directions.

Russian and Chinese tracer rounds use different chemical compounds that produce their green tracer. The Taliban probably thought they were getting hit by 'mosquitoes' – the name they had given to Apache gunships. However, they were being used tonight not to hunt but to protect the Chinooks. Their ammunition would be needed for the exfiltration if the Rangers lost the firefight.

Allen's team leader pulled his men together. 'She's not in here,' he told them. All the building's rooms had been searched. Four dead Taliban had been added to the furniture.

Of the hostage, there was no sign.

CHAPTER 3

The team leader in the second building came on the net. 'Building Two clear. We found signs of the hostage, but she's not here. There's a tunnel leading out. I'll send two down there. Team One, get outside the compound, start looking for the tunnel exit.'

'Roger. Out,' Allen's team leader replied into his radio. His name was Alex Banks, a Chief Petty Officer from Boulder, Colorado. At six foot two he was as tall as Allen, with a short beard and dark eyes. He was an experienced warrior and had the deep respect of his team. He led them now. 'On me,' was all that he needed to say.

They left the dead Taliban behind them and ran out into the compound. Allen saw an unbroken line of red in the sky, and heard the buzz once more of the AC-130's Gatling gun a split second later. The team ran for the compound's gate. Their explosives expert quickly checked it for improvised explosive devices, and when he found none, kicked it open.

Allen followed. A track led away into the forest. 'Split down into pairs,' Banks told them. 'I'll take the track. Tex, take to the left. Allen, take the right. Work around the compound. Go.'

Allen wasted no time and moved off with Miller, his weapon in the low ready. Allen had some experience with tunnels and he weighed up the factors to decide how close he would search to the compound. Tunnels could run for hundreds of metres, like they did under the Mexican/US border, but Allen reckoned that this one would exit close to the high compound walls. The mountain would be hard digging, especially given that it was threaded with the roots of thousands of trees. Their best bet was to find breaks in the forest. That was where the exit was most likely to be.

Thunderclaps boomed in the sky above Allen, but it was not the work of nature. The Angel of Death was now pumping 105mm artillery shells onto the opposite mountainside. Allen couldn't see them, but the noise of the explosions rolled through the valley. The Taliban were throwing everything they had at the Rangers' cordon, but the Rangers were giving as good as they got. They were firing, reloading, calling out targets, and painting the enemy firing positions with lasers for the Spectre gunship to lock on and engage.

The Rangers were riding adrenaline and fighting for their lives, but Allen and Miller were quietly stalking through the forest like men hunting deer. It was an eerie scene as the echoes of battle rattled through the trees, but Allen did all he could to block out the noise and focus on his search. Seen through his night vision, the forest was a collection of black shapes and shadows. Allen stepped quietly from one tree to the next, using them to cover his left side as he scanned ahead. He didn't have time to think about what could be under his feet.

It was estimated that the Russians laid over a million of their anti-personnel mines in Afghanistan; around

110 civilians a month were being killed by these 'legacy mines' since the Russian withdrawal in the 1980s. Tens of thousands were laid in Kunar Province, particularly in the Korengal. This place had always been the Valley of Death. Allen had seen what they could do, but there wasn't anything he could do that would prevent him from stepping on one. He had a job to do, he just had to crack on.

And then he saw them.

It was only a glimpse, but Allen was sure of what he'd seen through his night vision. Fifty metres ahead, the silhouette of a head and shoulders had appeared above the ground for a few seconds, then vanished from sight.

Miller had stopped when Allen had. Allen looked in the American's direction, pointed to his own eyes and gave a thumbs down. Allen used an infrared laser module to briefly paint the part of the ground where he'd seen the movement, then turned the laser off quickly. In the fog of war, it was possible that the Spectre systems would mistake it for a target indication.

Allen began creeping forward, his weapon in the high ready. He'd barely taken 10 steps when a figure emerged from the ground, quickly followed by another. They had no idea how close he was, or that they'd been seen. Both men were carrying AK-47s, and Allen had to assume that they'd be wearing suicide vests too. He silently went to one knee, and watched. He wouldn't fire. Not until he was sure that they were all out of there.

The next person didn't climb out of the hole: they were pulled. That could mean one of two things: it was either a wounded fighter that they were lifting or it was the hostage.

Allen kept his breath steady. Beneath the cover of the trees it was difficult to make out features, and the nearby firefight and air support ruined any chance he had of hearing voices, but then he saw *something*. It was the hostage's hair that gave it away. As she was pulled out of the hole she recoiled from her captors. As she did, Allen saw a ponytail flick back. No man in Afghanistan had a ponytail.

Allen wasted no more time.

He gently squeezed the trigger and put a round through the head of one of the men. Miller had been waiting, and his own shot took the second man down. They dropped to the ground like falling trees and then the woman was running. Allen was about to sprint after her when a third shape emerged from the hole, an AK in hand that he aimed in the direction of the fleeing hostage. He didn't even see Allen and died with two rounds in the back of his head. Allen waited for more of the enemy to emerge from the hole.

A grenade came flying out instead.

CHAPTER 4

'Grenade!'

The explosion sent splinters flying from the trees and showered Allen in cold dirt. The Taliban fighter had courage, and was up into a firing position and spraying three-round bursts a second later. This wasn't the 'spray and pray' of an amateur, but the accurate fire of a seasoned fighter who knew his business.

Allen and Miller fired back, but the fighter dropped back into the hole. He must have reckoned that to appear again was to die, and now only his AK appeared over the rim of the tunnel mouth. He compensated for the lack of accuracy with longer bursts. A lucky shot was as deadly as an aimed one, and rounds chewed the trunks of the trees close to Allen's head.

Allen swore to himself and got on the net. 'All call signs this is Redcoat.' His call sign had been jokingly given to the Brit in their team. 'Hostage last seen moving south, alone. We're taking fire and can't move. Over.'

'Redcoat' – Banks on the net – 'can you direct air? Over.'

'Negative. The hostage might have taken cover close by.'

'Roger that. Tex, keep pushing around, see if you can sweep her up. Over.'

'Roger. Out.'

'Redcoat,' Banks went on, 'fight through and close in with Tex. Out.'

'Miller!' Allen shouted over the gunfire. 'Keep the fucker's head down! I'll go in!'

There was no need for Miller to shout a reply. His firing did the talking, a steady stream of rapid single shots that chewed up the lip of the tunnel hole. Allen began crawling forward across the forest floor, ignoring the pain of the sharp stones that bit into his arms and legs. Miller fired a double tap as the AK appeared and quickly withdrew.

'Stoppage!' Miller shouted.

Allen stopped and took up the firing himself. It didn't matter what had caused the stoppage, a mag change or problems with the working parts, fire had to be maintained at the target while Miller sorted out his weapon. Allen was within 20 metres now, and the chances of a Taliban lucky shot got higher the closer he crawled to the hole.

Miller began to fire again. Allen changed magazines as he crawled. He was within five metres. Close enough. He took a baseball-shaped M67 hand grenade from a pouch, popped the safety clip off the handle, known as the spoon, and gripped the grenade and spoon hard before pulling the pin. He gently lobbed it into the tunnel and heard the *ping* as the spoon flew away from the grenade and the internal spring armed the weapon. If it landed on the surface it would be far more dangerous to him than the enemy, and as he saw it drop away into the hole Allen felt like he'd thrown the winning shot in the NBA finals.

Allen waited the four to five seconds before it detonated. With a fatal area of five metres he knew it would clear the tunnel for him.

Two seconds later, the grenade came flying back out. The fighter was close enough to also hear the *ping* and had the experience and the bollocks to do something about it. Now it was Allen who would be on the receiving end.

Allen pushed his face into the cold ground to protect his eyes. He didn't see it explode a metre in the air above the hole, but he felt something hit him in the back. There was no time to think if he was injured now. Allen sprung up from the ground, rushed to the hole, and poured a magazine into it on automatic. When the bolt stayed back he let the weapon fall on its sling to his side, and drew the pistol and maintained the rate of fire.

Miller ran up beside him, pulled the pin, then threw another M67 in hard.

The explosion detonated beneath the ground.

Miller was relieved. 'No one else is coming out of there.' Allen was getting up as quickly. 'You hit?'

'Aye.'

'Bad?'

'Still breathing. Let's push on.'

They got to their feet just as another explosion echoed through the forest. 'Mine? Maybe grenade?' Miller asked.

'One of them. It's not Spectre. Too small.'

Allen felt a sick feeling in his stomach.

The explosion had come from the south, where the hostage had been running.

• • •

She lay very still. The ground about her had been pushed away by the mine's detonation, along with the lower part of her right leg, just below the knee.

There was nothing to be said by the two operators. They knew what to do.

Tex grabbed his trauma kit, pulled out a tourniquet and started applying it above the knee of the shattered leg. Plug the leaking and keep them breathing or they die. There was nothing difficult or special about it in the field; it was just bloody and hands-on. Casualties had to be gripped if they were to be saved.

Allen knelt beside her, his face nearly touching the bloody mess that was hers. The skin on the left-hand side flapped open to expose her gumline. He couldn't feel any breath coming from her on his skin. He couldn't see any chest movement. Allen lifted one of her eyelids and shone his torch. No pupil reaction. Nothing anywhere to show she was alive. But that didn't matter; Allen knew he still had a job to do until it was obvious they had been too late.

He turned her onto her side as Tex finished twisting the plastic handle on the tourniquet to put pressure around her leg to stop the blood flow.

Allen opened her lips and dug his fingers into her mouth to scoop out a couple of broken teeth, then a big plug of mucus and blood that was blocking her airway. Fuck wasting time finding out if she had a pulse. Allen needed to breathe for her, fill her lungs with air. Even if her heart was still pumping, it was doing nothing without oxygen.

He rolled her onto her back again, tilting her head back to open the airway as Tex got on the net.

'We found her. She's a CAT A. Say again we have a CAT A.'

Allen left Tex to talk the support in.

She was warm and the only real dead body is a cold one.

Allen eased her head back to open the airway, pinched her nose shut with his right hand and held together the rip in her cheek with his left.

Allen filled his lungs and put his mouth over what was left of hers, tasting the metallic tang of her blood as he breathed into her.

It wasn't working. He could feel some of his breath leaking through the rip in her cheek and past his fingers, but her chest rose a fraction. He tried again, holding the cheek wound firmer, but it was no good. His left hand was slipping on her blood-drenched skin. He couldn't keep a good enough seal. Her blood dripped out of Allen's mouth as he called out for Tex. 'Get over here! Keep this fucking rip together.'

The American came and knelt beside him and gripped the rip with both hands as Allen took a deep breath, got as good a seal as he could around her mouth and exhaled.

Her chest rose. She was taking in oxygen. Allen breathed into her again.

Ten big breaths to get her inflated, spitting out her blood between each one as Tex fought to keep her skin sealed. Allen could still feel air leaking through her cheek, but it was working. Somewhere in his brain he was also crying out for oxygen.

Ten done, and Allen now checked for a pulse. Jamming two fingers into the side of her neck he found her carotid.

Nothing. She was still only getting oxygen from him, and her heart wasn't pumping any of that oxygenated blood around her body.

It was the first time Allen had said anything since getting Tex to help.

'Shit.'

He hoped nothing was fractured in her chest area, because if it was and a fractured rib penetrated an organ, what he was going to do next might kill her. But if he didn't do anything she would be dead anyway.

Allen put the heel of his left hand onto her sternum, and his right on top of that, leaned over her, straightened his arms and started pumping steadily with his body weight, pressing straight down by five to six centimetres, counting off the beats in his head: twice a second.

One, two, three, four, five ... one, two, three, four, five ...

He spat out another mouthful of blood and started to call it out loud: 'One, two, three, four, five ... one, two, three, four, five ...'

Tex was putting a second tourniquet just above the first because it hadn't stopped the leaking.

'Tex, squeeze her face together again – we need that seal.'

He dropped to his knees.

Allen got his mouth round hers, pinched her nose and breathed hard. Fuck knows how long it had been since her brain had last had oxygen.

Her lungs fully inflated this time. Once. Twice. Then it was back to 30 pumps over her heart.

One, two, three, four, five ... one, two, three, four, five ...

Head back, two more breaths.

In Allen's head the world had closed in and was a whole lot quieter now. No Ranger contacts, no AC-130 Gatling guns buzzing, just his own breath as he concentrated on trying to save this woman.

One, two, three, four, five ... one, two, three, four, five ...

He pumped away, six cycles of five compressions, squashing the heart to move that oxygenated blood round her body. A fair amount of red stuff was oozing out of her from general, smaller wounds, but it wasn't as bad as it looked. If you drop a bottle of ketchup on your kitchen floor it looks like breakfast has turned into the Texas chainsaw massacre, but it's only one bottle. The leg, that was the problem.

'Start breathing, for fuck's sake! One, two, three, four, five ... one, two, three, four, five ...'

Nothing. Not a flicker.

Tex dug fingers into her neck for a pulse. 'Nothing.'

'But she's still warm, keep that face sealed, keep it closed.'

Allen had just started to give her more oxygen when the medics dropped to their knees beside him and took over. Allen and Tex sat against a tree, too fucked and depressed to wipe away her blood from their hands and kit as they watched the medics try to revive her.

But it was a waste of time.

CHAPTER 5

KANDAHAR, AFGHANISTAN, 2012

Sergeant Harry Allen was happy to be back in Afghanistan, even if it wasn't at the rank he'd hoped to have achieved at this point in his career.

What had happened in the Korengal still played out in his head. The fact that the hostage had died and so the mission was a failure wasn't the problem.

Things happen in the battlespace that aren't planned or foreseen. Being in 'the fight' isn't a science. Mistakes are made and must be dealt with on the ground as they happen. A German strategist had coined the term 'the fog of war' for good reason. Sometimes winning was just a case of who made the fewest errors. That night in the Korengal, the insertion had gone to plan, and the kidnappers had been taken down without a single fatality to the rescue force. Among the Taliban dead were two well-known commanders, but this hadn't been a raid to cut heads off the snake. It had been a mission to rescue a hostage, and the hostage had died of the wounds she had sustained. Wounds that weren't caused by the Taliban, but by a fragmentation grenade thrown by a Navy SEAL. The harsh reality is that people die in war. Dead combatants and civilians have always been the end result of lethal encounters. Soldiers understand that, and often wish that the civilians who send them to war did too. But those people didn't really understand; they just wanted results. Good results. Allen understood that the death of a Western civilian here amplified calls to 'bring our troops and people home'.

Every death brought more scrutiny in the Western newspapers, and more calls for action: particularly the action of leaving the country. It had been more than 11 years since NATO had come to Afghanistan. Most people hadn't been expecting the war to go on for 11 months, let alone for more than a decade, but fresh troops had rotated in and out of Afghanistan as regular as clockwork, and their numbers had surged. The plan was to eventually hand over all combat operations to the Afghan Security Forces, but from Allen's experience that day was a long way away. What really kept the Taliban on its heels were special forces raids and air strikes, but both were a double-edged sword. There were a lot of complaints about raids in the middle of the night, and a lot of civilian deaths from bombs. It was possible that NATO might beat the enemy but lose the support of the population, which would only guarantee that the enemy would resurge, and win in the end. There were few certainties in war, but calls to pull the military away from conflict was one of them.

But that was their problem. Allen's was different, more personal. He had experienced friends die in his arms. They were soldiers, they had signed the non-liability contract to fight, and that had helped ease the pain for him. But the woman was a civilian, who had just wanted to help other civilians caught up in this war. He thought these people were crazy to do so, yet at the same time, he felt admiration for their fearless commitment to save lives. He had never met any of these people before that night, and her death was a loss for Allen. He couldn't explain to himself why, but he felt it and never wanted to have the same feeling again.

But that was then and this was now. Allen was now back with the regiment and sitting in the passenger seat of an old Nissan Sunny that would have given an MOT mechanic a heart attack. The vehicle had once been white, but now it was beige with dust, and covered in dents and bumps. It wasn't the kind of vehicle to turn heads in Kandahar, and that was the point ...

Allen was undercover. He wore a blue-coloured dish-dasha and a turban in a darker shade. His beard and skin, already dark, had dye and make-up applied to make him look darker still. The man beside him didn't need help with his disguise. Mohammed, known as 'Mo', was an Afghan Commando who had been fighting the Taliban constantly for seven years. He'd been shot twice in the process, and lost a brother to a Taliban death squad. While Western soldiers like Allen got to go home for years between tours, there were no breaks for the Afghan Commandos. As well as being constantly at war, their families lived in danger. If the Taliban could find a commando or his family, then they would murder them in the most brutal of ways. They often sent videos of the murders to contacts in the victim's phone. They were fighting a war of terror, but Allen and Mo planned on fighting it back.

Raids were exciting, but for Allen it was hard to match the excitement of driving through an enemy-controlled town, almost alone, and gaining information on the enemy

33

from right under their own noses. This was the secretive work of the special forces which was rarely seen: building the intelligence picture. Without intelligence, there could be no raids. Intelligence was any army's or terror group's most powerful weapon.

Today, Allen's target was a Taliban commander by the name of Siddiqi. Intelligence sources had reported that Siddiqi was leaving Helmand Province, where his attacks had been responsible for dozens of British, American and Afghan deaths. The reports reckoned that Siddiqi was coming to Kandahar for a meeting, and the guess was that he would be meeting someone higher up the Taliban's chain of command. Everyone took their orders from someone. If they could find Siddiqi, they could find his meeting, raid it and put a dent in the Taliban's operational command.

'The next right,' Mo said quietly in English.

Allen didn't reply. Words were kept to the bare minimum while working undercover. The traffic in Kandahar was chaotic, with everyone following their own rules, and the noise was enough to easily drown out whispers, but the human mind was surprisingly good at picking up lip movements that weren't familiar. Located in the Pashtun-dominated south of the country, Kandahar had long been a base of support for the Taliban. Every man on the street could be part of the organisation or sympathetic to the cause. Allen's head was in the lion's mouth.

As Mohammed turned into the next road, Allen's luck ran out.

CHAPTER 6

Allen didn't waste time cursing his luck when he saw the Taliban checkpoint: that would have been to waste time that he didn't have. Five cars ahead of their Sunny, two pickup trucks were pulled across the road, staggered to allow traffic through, but only at a crawl. Two Taliban fighters stood in the pickup trucks looking over the scene. A half-dozen more were milling about in the traffic. Illegal vehicle checkpoints (IVCPs) like this were a common part of insurgencies. From Belfast to Baghdad, insurgents liked to show the locals 'who is boss'. Officers may have had coloured-in maps saying that they controlled an area, but that meant nothing to a local who had to face armed men on their way to work. Usually, the greatest danger was to the locals' wallets, not their lives, as the Taliban and other groups would use these IVCPs to extract bribes. Some of this money would be passed up the chain to support the war effort, but some would go into the fighters' pockets. Not every Talib waged jihad for religious reasons; many did it because Afghanistan's economy was nearly non-existent. For them, like many of the Western soldiers whom they fought against, they had joined an armed force because they needed a job.

Allen made a quick assessment of the situation. He didn't see anyone being pulled out of their cars and whipped for transgressions to sharia law, such as being clean shaven, and this gave him confidence that the Taliban ahead of him were there to shake down the locals, not make them 'better Muslims'. That didn't mean that they weren't part of the security pickets for Siddiqi. The Taliban commander was reckoned to be less than a K further down this road, and because of the checkpoint, Allen thought there was a good chance that this was true.

There was still time and space to tell Mo to turn the car, and leave quickly in the opposite direction, but Allen didn't give the order. If these men were here because of Siddiqi he didn't want to spook them. They would go through the Taliban checkpoint.

Allen looked at Mo and gave him a confident nod. There was no need to talk. They had trained for this for a reason. Mo lightly touched the accelerator, and the Sunny crept forward with the traffic.

Some of the cars ahead of them went through faster than others. Anything from 20 seconds to two minutes. Allen reckoned this was down to who paid up quickly, and who pleaded poverty until finally giving in and handing over the money. No one had been asked to get out. If the Taliban gave that order to Allen, he would comply, but when he did it would be with a Heckler & Koch snub-nosed MP5K in his hands. The weapon was under his seat, and there was more armament hidden in the vehicle's boot: an anti-armour missile to destroy their own car, and the covert communications equipment that it carried.

As they inched forward, Allen kept his head still but let his eyes roam, searching for any Taliban who weren't obvious. Had they positioned men on the rooftops? Were there cut-off groups, like a British army VCP would put in place? In the side mirror, a car caught Allen's eye. It hadn't turned into the road, but positioned itself on the main road so that it could look down it. Allen heard a familiar, quiet voice in the earpiece that was hidden beneath his turban.

'Are you compromised?' the Welsh voice asked him.

Allen pressed a hidden pressle on his radio once for no.

'Do you want us to hold here?' the voice asked again.

Allen pressed it twice for yes. If a fight ensued, he and Mo would fire and manoeuvre back to the second car while the SAS soldiers inside it would drive to get closer to the pair, get their anti-armour out to destroy the Sunny and so slow everybody down so that they could pick up Allen and Mo, and then drive out of the area as fast as they could. It would be a dirty dash: there wasn't anything clean about close-quarter combat, even when things went perfectly.

There was only one car ahead of them now. Allen got a better look at the Taliban who were manning the checkpoint. One of the reasons he loved this kind of work was that it let him see his enemy up close when they weren't shooting at him. The men standing in the pickups looked bored and tired by the heat. The ones talking to the car ahead smiled now and then, like they were doing the locals a favour. Maybe they were. The Taliban wouldn't have been able to hold on for this long in the war if no one in the local population supported them. Some would do so out of fear. Others for ideological reasons. Afghanistan had a history of kicking out 'invaders' for a reason. They were a proud people, and many hated the idea of a distant, foreign government such as America's shaping their country.

The car ahead of them was waved on and moved slowly through the chicane of the two pickups. Calm and collected, Mo put the car into first gear and moved forward. It was time for him and Allen to act out the roles they'd rehearsed. No one had told Allen that he'd need acting skills to be a special forces soldier, but at times like this the ability to play a role was as useful as marksmanship.

Mo came to a stop and rolled down his window. '*As-salaam alaikum!*' he said cheerfully.

'*Wa alaikum assalaam,*' the Taliban fighter replied with a smile. His teeth were yellow and his beard was dark and scraggly. Allen didn't look his way. He kept staring forward out of the window, as though he had no idea where he was. His role was to pretend to be Mohammed's idiot cousin.

Mo and the checkpoint commander continued speaking in Pashtun. Allen couldn't understand a word of it, but the tone seemed happy, and there was even a laugh from the Talib. Allen felt Mo's hand on his. This was the part of the act where Mo would put on the sob story, telling the Taliban fighters how Allen was an idiot. A burden on the family, but family nonetheless. Allen stayed as still as a statue as Mo then leaned across him, opened the glove boxes, and reached in to take out some loose currency in the local denomination. As he handed it over, Allen caught the same word a few times: 'Allah.' No doubt Mo was praising the Taliban as holy warriors of god, feigning happiness to be putting money in their pockets.

Allen felt a shape appear in the window beside him. He didn't look. He couldn't. Mo was the local national, and it was on his judgement to decide when things had gone past the point of saving and to initiate the contact. Mo was a highly respected commando, and Allen had no worry that he would act out of fear. The Afghan had nerves of steel, and they held now. He laughed again, thanked the Taliban like an old friend, and put the car into gear. Slowly, slowly, they crept through the enemy's chicane. Then, the road ahead of them was clear. Mo drove on for 10 seconds before he felt they were in the clear enough to speak, and grinned.

'You play a great idiot, Allen. You must have had many years of practice.'

CHAPTER 7

BADAKHSHAN PROVINCE

Laura Jones looked at the young mother in front of her and wished that she could do more. They were in a poorly lit room made of mudbrick, situated within thick compound walls, a testament to the perpetual war in the region. The young mother cradled a sick infant in her arms, though the child's fever looked like breaking after the medicine that Laura had given her had taken effect. The child would live, but for how long was anyone's guess. There were a lot of ways to die in Afghanistan.

Laura was not ignorant of the dangers of life here. In fact, it was these very dangers that had compelled her to be in Afghanistan, and in Badakhshan Province in particular. Badakhshan was one of the world's most impoverished places, and with poverty came crime and disease. It was often the most vulnerable who suffered, including children. Laura was not a mother, but she was a woman and a human being, and she couldn't stomach the idea that there were children dying in Afghanistan while she was safe in the UK. Just like many of the soldiers who came to fight the Taliban, Laura was willing to risk her own life to try and make a better life for strangers.

Laura had taken a position in an NGO, whose aim was to reduce child mortality. In 1990 an Afghan child had a one in five chance of dying before they were five years old. Thanks to organisations like the programme that Laura worked for, that number had been cut by two thirds. It was still tragically high, but things were moving in the right direction.

The English woman wasn't alone in her mission. Adele was in her thirties, around the same age as Laura, and had come from her home in Kenya to help in the war-torn country. Laura also worked with two women from Herat, which lay to the south of Badakhshan and had been one of the most persecuted places under the Taliban's heel. Once the misogynistic regime had fallen, Tasneem and Zahab had enrolled in medical training to become midwives. In her late forties, Tasneem was old enough to be Zahab's mother. She was the matriarch of the group, acting as their guide, mentor, and now, their hope.

Tasneem walked into the room now. As ever she wore a patient, warm smile. She spoke a few words to the mother in Dari, Laura picking out the odd word – she was learning the tongue language slowly but surely – and then Tasneem spoke to her in accented but excellent English.

'I've seen to the other children, Laura. Adele and Zahab have the mules ready. We should leave now.'

'We're not staying the night?' Laura asked, looking at the child and anxious not to leave too soon. Tasneem understood her worry and comforted her.

'We've done our work here, now the medication will do the rest. The longer we stay, the less time there is for the children in the next village.'

'Yes,' Laura agreed. 'Yes, you're right.' She stood, smiled at the mother and gently placed her hand on her shoulder. There was no need for words. The young mother's eyes spoke of her thanks, and Laura's of her hope for this young family.

'Goodbye,' Laura said in Dari. 'We will be thinking of you.' They weren't empty words. Though they had helped dozens of children on this aid mission, Laura could remember the face of every one of them. It was impossible to forget them, or their mothers, though it felt like the world often did. So be it. Laura could not be accountable for every person's actions, only her own, and she knew in her heart that she was where she was supposed to be.

'Let's go,' she said to Tasneem.

Outside, the sun was high and harsh, and the villagers gathered in the shade of trees that ran beside a bubbling stream. The people were poor but their country was rich in beauty and hospitality. The villagers would not allow the aid workers to leave before they had eaten stew and flatbread. Laura watched a group of young boys playing with a football that had been punctured long ago, but there were smiles on their faces, and that put a smile on hers. Her heart hurt for these people. They had been through so much, and were going through so much still, but she had never met any people more generous, more kind than those of Afghanistan. She was not able to reconcile this treatment of guests with the perpetual war in the country, and she said as much to Afghanistan.

'It is because of war that we must be so kind,' Tasneem explained. 'We are at each other's mercy. We rely on the tradition of honouring and protecting guests, as well as family. The deep bonds and traditions that lead to wars and feuds are the same ones that mean we could give our last scrap of bread to a stranger in our home, even at the expense of our own children.'

'I don't understand it,' Laura replied.

Tasneem smiled. 'When you spend enough time here, you will. Come on,' she added, 'it's time we left.'

They mounted their mules and waved goodbye. Laura took one last look at the smiling boys kicking the football. It would be her last happy memory for a long time.

CHAPTER 8

Umid looked at the AK-47 in his hands, and smiled. To him, the weapon was a symbol that his time as a boy was nearly over.

Just like his father had been at 18, when he had taken up arms to fight the Soviet invaders. The youngest of eight siblings, two of whom had died as young children, Umid had always looked at his father with awe. He had been a warrior, and in their home, he was their provider, the judge, and the security against the dangers of the world. It had always been Umid's dream to emulate that man, and perhaps today would be the beginning of that.

Umid had lived all of his life in Fayzabad, a town of fewer than 40,000 people. Surrounded by mountains, and built along a wide, snaking river, Umid had always believed that his home was beautiful, and worth fighting for. He had considered joining both the Taliban and the forces of the Afghan Republic – he had family in both – but his father had forbidden it.

'There is no good in this war,' he had told his youngest son. 'I will not have you be a part of it.'

That settled the matter. A father's word was law, and Umid would obey. Still, if he was ever to have a family of his own, he needed money. The home of his father would pass to

Umid's oldest brother, and the economy in Badakhshan was next to non-existent. And so, Umid had asked his father's permission to take work for a local warlord. He would be fed and paid. His father was hesitant at first.

'Warlords can be bought. You could end up fighting for the Taliban, or against them. I fought in war so that my sons wouldn't have to.'

Umid had pleaded his case. In the end he'd promised his father that if the warlord threw in his lot with either side, then he would leave his employment and come home.

'Life isn't that simple,' his father had said but agreed anyway. Times were hard on them all. The family was growing, and money was dwindling. 'You have my blessing,' he said at last.

That had been four weeks ago. At first the warlord's men had turned Umid away, but when they learned who his father was, they welcomed him in. 'If you fight half as well as your father did, then you will be a great warrior.'

These words had come from Sherali, whose face was as lined as the mountains of Badakhshan, his beard long and thick and shot through with white. He was one of the warlord's most trusted commanders and carried his rifle like he had been born with it in his hands.

Umid was in awe of him, and overjoyed when Sherali had chosen him to accompany him on a mission along with a dozen other men.

'Where are we going?' Umid asked them as they packed weapons, ammunition and supplies.

'To earn our keep,' was all Sherali had said.

They had driven east, staying with cousins of the men in the party along the way. Finally they had made a camp, and Sherali left four men to guard it. The vehicles that had brought them drove away, and Sherali had laughed at Umid's puzzled expression.

'God gave you those for a reason,' he said, pointing at Umid's feet.

Since then his feet had blistered, then hardened. Sherali was half mountain goat, and didn't seem affected by the steep climbs through the mountains. At first Umid had wheezed, and in the morning every muscle had been sore, but he was young, and his body adapted quickly. After two weeks in the mountains, he felt as good as he had ever done. It was a joy to walk through his homeland, and he said as much to his leader.

'You might think differently in winter,' Sherali had said with a smile.

'What is it we're looking for?' Umid had asked him.

'We'll know when we find it,' was all the bandit said to that.

And today they had.

There were four of them, riding their mules up the valley floor without a care in the world. Unlike his father, Umid had never seen a person with white skin.

'Are they invaders?' he whispered to Sherali.

'Better,' the old bandit replied. 'They are a fortune.'

Umid was alone with Sherali on a craggy outcrop where the mountain pass narrowed. Umid didn't need to be an expert to see that the four riders in the valley would need to pass within metres of them to make their way through the steep-sided cliffs. The rest of Sherali's party had been scattered.

It was the animals that first knew something was amiss. They could smell the bandits, and while they didn't know what that smell meant, they knew enough to be cautious. One mule tossed its head. A second stopped and refused to go forward. A former mujahid and bandit like Sherali would have known what that meant, but the people on the mules' backs did not. They urged their animals forward. Forward into the trap.

Umid's heart beat faster. The sight of the strangers was part of the reason, but so was the word that Sherali had said: 'fortune'. Umid had expected it would be years before he would have enough money for a home and family. Maybe he could have his dream before he turned 19?

'Don't move until I do,' Sherali whispered, sensing Umid's excitement.

The mules came onwards. They were close enough now for Umid to see the women's features. He could hear their happy, idle conversation. They had no idea what was about to happen to them.

Sherali held an old battered radio to his lips. 'Now,' he said into it, closing the net.

There was no fight. No resistance. The four women were unarmed and the sight of the bandits sent them into frozen shock.

'I'm a British citizen,' one of them said in Dari.

Sherali laughed, and turned to Umid. 'What did I tell you, boy? Fortunes.'

CHAPTER 9

KABUL

Colin Miller felt the weight of his carbine in his hands, and double-checked the fit of his magazine. Since his last deployment to the country he had qualified as a SEAL breacher, an expert in explosives and other forms of gaining entry into places that the enemy didn't want you to get into. Now, when he felt a tap on his shoulder, Miller led the way forward through a winding entanglement of dark alleyways.

The sun had set an hour before. There was still the sound of traffic in the city. Dogs and car horns barked. Somewhere in the sky above them, a plane was leaving Hamid Karzai International Airport. It could have been the sounds of a city anywhere in the world, but here, and now, a force of DEVGRU SEALs and Afghan Commandos were closing the noose around the necks of one of their enemies.

Unlike a lot of the country where they had fought, the buildings in Kabul resembled those of a normal city more than they did the thick mud-walled compounds of Afghanistan's rural provinces. Some of the houses had walls topped with broken glass and barbed wire, but the SEALs' target was a four-storey building with a door that opened straight on to a street. Perhaps the men inside, affiliates of Al-Qaeda, had hoped that they would draw less attention in a more lightly defended building. In that they had been wrong. The vast intelligence network in the city had tracked and pinpointed them to here, and the Pentagon had weighed up options. A drone strike had been considered to safeguard the lives of SEALs, but the building was in a built-up area, and the likelihood of collateral damage, a more clinical and less emotional way of saying civilian casualties in an air strike, was high. The SEALs' commanders had lobbied for their men to be the ones to take out the threat and had received the green light earlier that day.

Miller had studied everything he could about the breach point. He wasn't going to take his team into the funnel of a door, but make his own in the side of the building. And so he had studied the intelligence: how thick were the walls? What were they made of? Were they reinforced? All of this information he used to make an explosive charge that would blow a hole in the side of the building without bringing the whole thing down on the top of his teammates' heads. Their lives were in his hands, and he would not let them down.

With his weapon in the high ready, Miller stalked forward, tight to the wall. Behind him his teammates covered other angles, some at the high windows, others across the street. The moving team looked like a battleship bristling with weapons.

Miller came to his entry point, let his carbine hang gently on its sling, and peeled off the adhesive side of the charge and placed it against the wall. He took a couple of steps back, unrolling the wiring attached to the charge's detonator as he went, and waited for the command.

It came across the radio a few heartbeats later.

'Execute-execute-execute.'

CHAPTER 10

The roar of the explosion echoed through the street, a cloud of dust and debris billowing outwards. A nearby car alarm was set off, the street's dogs started barking wildly, and parents in the houses called for their children and pulled them into cover.

Miller ignored all those distractions. He was already moving through the entry point with his rifle held up in front of him. The room looked like any living room in the world, but the sofa was now turned on its side and pictures had been blown off the walls. Through the green of his night-vision goggles Miller saw movement in a doorway to his right. He ignored everything about the man except what was in his hands.

A weapon.

Miller fired three times. Two centre mass of the target. Then one into the man's skull as he lay crumpled on the tiled floor, to ensure he would no longer be a threat.

'Door right! Door front! Room clear!' Miller shouted as he skirted by the sofa.

'Take door right!' his team commander called. Miller moved into the doorway and arched from his hips so that the minimum amount of his upper body showed. His IR laser pointed straight up a staircase finding another armed man. Miller flicked his select lever to auto and drilled two three-round bursts into the man's chest, the terrorist falling onto his back then sliding down the stairway like a bobsled.

'I'm taking the stairs!' Miller called, knowing that time was of the essence.

'Stun out!' someone behind him shouted, and through his night vision he saw two canisters sail onto the upper landing then explode, the flashes whiting out his night vision for a moment, the sound ringing in his ears. But Miller had trained for this environment and the enemy hadn't. An AK appeared around a doorway, firing wildly. The man thought he was safe behind the wall, but it was not thick enough to stop the rounds that Miller and the SEAL behind him drilled through it. Another AK dropped useless to the floor.

Three down. Their intelligence had reported that there were three terrorists in their supposed safe house, but Miller and the SEALs took no chances, sweeping each room with unrelenting precision. Eventually, there were no more rooms left to clear.

'Upstairs clear!' Miller shouted, and a few moments later they got the call over the radio. The words that let them know that the takedown was over.

'All secure, all secure.'

CHAPTER 11

BAGRAM AIRBASE

After a successful DEVGRU raid earlier in the night, Federico Vasquez should have been happy, but the American was troubled. Very troubled. Vasquez worked for 'the company', which was a polite way of saying that he was a CIA agent, working in the 'off the books' side of Afghanistan's war.

Vasquez had a shaved head, a suggestion of his wife's once he'd started prematurely balding. He also agreed with her that he should stop smoking, yet still he took a cigarette from the packet of Newports and lit it, eventually flicking ash into an ashtray that was made from the base of an artillery shell casing. The third thing he had agreed was that he should look after himself more, maybe lose a couple of pounds. Vasquez may have felt weak for not being able to give up nicotine and snacks, but the 40-year-old was no one's idea of soft. Vasquez's office was a reflection of his work. There were no windows and no clutter. It was strictly business. Clandestine business.

There was a knock at the door.

'Yo. It's open.'

Taller than Vasquez, Rachael Powell had the fit athletic physique of someone who had spent much of their life on horseback. The 42-year-old's hair was tied back in a no-nonsense ponytail, a style that hadn't changed for her since her childhood at boarding school. The only difference now was the few strands of grey. Powell was Vasquez's British opposite number, and had got to know him well. Well enough to call him a lard-arse for not going to the gym with her and to be able to read his expression.

'Shit. What's happened?'

He waited until she'd closed the door, then offered her a cigarette. Rachael was his smoking partner in crime; they were both trying to give them up but both were so happy that the other one hadn't yet. As the smoke curled up and swirled beneath the ceiling fan, Vasquez brought her into the loop.

'A few days ago, one of my agent handlers in the north-east said that a warlord was planning to abduct a team of aid workers.'

'Shit,' she said firmly. 'When?'

'Already taken.'

Powell took a deep drag on her own cigarette. 'Do we know who? How many?'

'No, but the good news is that the source is confident they're still alive. They say it's a ransom job, and not affili-ated to the Taliban or Al-Qaeda. They want money, not murder videos, that's my guess.'

'Any idea on the nationalities?' Powell asked.

'So far no aid organisation has raised an alarm. My guys are going over any US aid workers in the north that we have registered, and checking in with their NGOs. Could you do the same with the Brits?'

'Of course,' she said, then went quiet.

'What?'

'I think we should speak to the command,' Powell said. 'If we have Americans and Brits in the mix, you know what they're like. Everything's a combined op under them, at least as far as possible. I think we should give a warning order to the SAS in Kandahar. Get them to send a hostage rescue team up here. You said the northeast, right?'

'Yeah. Badakhshan.'

'That fucking province.' Powell shook her head. 'Ten aid workers have been killed in the last two years.'

Vasquez nodded. 'And yet still they go.' He grunted. 'How much do you know about Badakhshan?'

'Most of my sources and work are in Helmand, Kandahar and Kabul. Badakhshan isn't really on the British radar.'

'You want to learn more about it?'

'Looks like I'm going to have to, doesn't it?'

'Yes it does.' Vasquez stubbed out his cigarette. 'We can walk and talk. Let's go and give the bad news to the big chiefs, shall we?'

CHAPTER 12

KANDAHAR

Sergeant Harry Allen swayed with the rhythm of the truck as they drove through the streets. He was no longer dressed as a local but kitted out in the Crye-cam that was the mark of the special forces, a lightweight helmet and night-vision goggles on his head, and a carbine cradled between his arms. Five other special forces soldiers rode with him in the back of the truck, which was as beat up and indistinguishable as the Sunny that he'd shared with Mo. The Afghan would also be a part of this night's work, but he would be leading in a team of commandos. Wherever possible, NATO's commanders in Afghanistan wanted special forces missions to be a joint effort between Western and local soldiers. This, it was hoped, would convince the locals that the out-of-country soldiers were here to support the Afghan government, and not as invaders. Looking ahead, it was also part of the exit plan so that the Afghan National Army would be capable once NATO had left the country.

Allen felt pride at what had happened that day. After passing the Taliban checkpoint, he and Mo had managed to pass the building suspected of housing the Taliban commander Siddiqi and the meeting he was hosting. They had driven by only once, but it had been enough to notice lookouts and an armed fighter. Based on this information,

Joint Special Operations Command (JSOC) had greenlit a mission to hit the building that same night. Allen would lead one of the assault teams, and his orders were clear: capture or kill Siddiqi, and any other Taliban who were on the target. With luck, they might sweep up the man who gave Siddiqi his orders.

It had been a long day for Allen, but no trace of tiredness touched him. He was about to lead five of his brothers into combat. Coffee didn't come close.

'Two minutes,' came over the radio net.

Allen pulled his night-vision goggles into place as the truck began to gently slow. This was no high-speed insertion like the failed mission in the Korengal Valley. The three teams would be dropped into place from trucks out of sight of lookouts, who were being watched by drones circling high in the sky. Too high to be heard or seen. Call sign Charlie would move into a position of fire support, and two more teams would assault. Allen's team, Alpha, would take the ground floor, and Bravo had an extendable ladder and would hit the target from the top. They'd squeeze the Taliban between them. If any should manage to escape, a force of Afghan Commandos were inbound by helicopter to form a perimeter as soon as the first shot was taken. Those same helicopters would then be used to extract the force and any prisoners.

'De-bus,' the mission's commander said over the radio.

Allen opened the truck's compartment door a few inches, looked through the gap, and stepped out onto the deserted street. In the day the city had been bustling with pedestrian and foot traffic, but now it was more like a ghost town. The locals knew what happened at night. So did the Taliban. None of them wanted to be caught out of cover by NATO's elite forces.

The sergeant took up a firing position in the corner of an alleyway and waited until his team were complete behind him. Standard operating procedure was to have a lead scout in front of him, but Allen had driven these roads and would lead them in himself. He understood the reason why a commander shouldn't always be at the front, but the warrior in him had never liked it.

Allen moved off quickly but carefully. The alleyways were full of the unpleasant stink of rotting food and open sewers. More than one soldier had fallen into neck-deep pits of shit, and Allen didn't plan on doing the same. It wasn't that he was scared of getting his hands dirty, but the filth carried sickness and could render a man incapable of being on duty.

From studying aerial photos, and rehearsing at their base on Kandahar Airfield, Allen knew exactly where he was going, and how long it would take him. When his team got into their final position, it was almost to the second of what he'd planned.

'That's Alpha at the start line.'

Allen got some satisfaction that it was almost a minute later before the two other teams reported the same. Outside of the city, Chinooks laden with Afghan Commandos would be taking off and heading their way. Apaches would be riding shotgun. It was now or never, before the noise of the helicopters alerted their prey.

'Alpha and Bravo, move now,' the commander ordered across the radio, and Allen led his team silently forward.

Unlike in Helmand Province, where Allen had conducted many raids, there weren't thick compound walls here. The Kandahar street could have fitted in most developed countries, the building a three-storey house surrounded by a six-foot wall topped with glass, easily overcome by laying a thick rubber mat across it. In no time, Allen's team were stacked up beside a side door, and he took his position behind the first pair of assaulters.

'Alpha ready,' he said, barely above a whisper.

'Bravo ready.'

'All call signs – I have control. Stand by ... stand by ... *go!*'

In the building, Allen heard panicked shouts coming from upstairs. An explosive entry was a great way to put the shits up someone, and the Taliban in the building would be left in no doubt who was coming for them now. One way or another, their war was over.

Flash-bangs boomed and blinded with white light. Allen's pointman dropped one man with a triple tap of bullets, and then did the same to another. From his position in the stack, Allen directed his team to take rooms.

'Taff, go left! Robbo, H, room to the front!'

More noise came from upstairs. The second assault team had breached and were killing from above. The SAS ran through the house like water, washing away any resistance.

'Al, over here!' one of his troopers called. He had his carbine in the face of a man on his knees. Allen knew from the photos in his intelligence brief that this was Siddiqi.

Allen got on to his radio and sent the code word: 'Jackpot, jackpot, jackpot'.

They had their man.

CHAPTER 13

Less than an hour later the Chinooks touched down at Kandahar Airfield (KAF) and the SAS stepped off onto the tarmac. Most headed straight to the debriefing room, anxious to get it over with. A few of them wanted to sleep, but Allen knew that others had more urgent reasons to get to their single man rooms: KAF was home to a large number of NATO militaries, and among them were female service members. The SAS were the alpha males of the base, and while there were no clubs to pick up women, there were coffee shops, gyms and dining halls. A few of the men had developed serious relationships, while others were trying out as many nationalities as they could. None of it interested Allen. He'd just come out the other side of a divorce. His wife didn't like the months of being alone while he was on operations and decided life with a property developer was more to her taste. Allen had come to Afghanistan just to fight, and his idea of a good night was leading a captured Taliban commander off the Chinook in plasticuffs and handing him over to the interrogators.

When this was done, Allen joined the others in the briefing room where they went over details of the mission: Was anything found on the target that could be useful for intelligence? What went well? What could have been done better? The debriefs often lasted longer than the missions themselves, and by the time that it was all over, Allen's adrenaline was a distant memory. After a long day, he was ready for his bed.

This wasn't going to happen.

The squadron sergeant major (SSM), Barry Taylor, entered the room. He looked like a surly sixth-former but had a warm personality. Allen hoped to have his job one day.

'Lads, we got a fast ball,' the SSM told them. 'You're all flying to Bagram as soon as we get the kit on board the wockas,' he added, using the nickname for the Chinook helicopters.

'What's going on, Baz?' Allen asked.

'No idea, but the warning order came from Kabul, so whatever it is, I doubt it's an invitation to dinner.'

CHAPTER 14

It had been a busy night for Allen and the other men. After the debriefing they had loaded the Chinooks inside and also prepared underslung loads. There were no exact details about what their mission might be, and so many eventualities had to be catered for. In the end, the SSM had come back and told them to get a shower and some sleep. 'We'll stand down until last light. Get a good rest, lads. I don't know what exactly they're giving us but it's going to be busy.'

Allen agreed. Usually their missions came down with intelligence reports and clear objectives. This had been different. A simple order to come to Bagram and prepare to stage operations from there. Was this how the US Navy SEALs had felt when they'd first been assembled in 2011, none of them knowing at first that they were going after the arch enemy himself, Osama bin Laden? He was the biggest trophy kill of all, but there were many more heads to cut from the snakes. Bagram was in the middle of Afghanistan. It could be used as a launch pad into anywhere in the country, or into neighbouring countries such as Pakistan.

Allen told himself that speculation could wait. Everything would be made clear at the right time. Until then he would clean his weapon, prep his kit and prep his body.

Food, water, shower, bed. Allen didn't know why they were going to Bagram, but something told him that the mission was going to take everything that he had.

CHAPTER 15

After dark the men boarded the helicopters. There was still no word about what lay ahead of them, but there was a buzz in the air, as though the soldiers were taking a bus to a cup final.

Allen took a seat on the Chinook's troop benches and made himself as comfortable as he could, which wasn't very. The CH-47s flew at high altitude, and cold wind rushed through the cabin from the open side doors.

'Shut the fucking doors!' someone shouted. 'Oi! Door gunner! Shut the fucking door!'

The trooper was ignored. Allen's guess was that the door gunners had their orders to stay in their positions, even on a joyride like this. At this altitude, their only danger was from mechanical malfunction or a bird strike. That put a little smile on Allen's face. To have come all this way, endured so much, fought so much, just to be killed by a goose in an aircraft engine. That would be some irony.

Despite the cold, and the threat of anti-aircraft geese, Allen fell asleep. When he woke they were touching down in Kabul, and with the other men he filed off the aircraft and stretched his arms to loosen his back. A few of the troopers were yawning. A couple of the more excitable ones were all smiles.

'Why are you so happy?' Allen asked Taff, one of the younger men who had come to them from an infantry regiment. It was Taff who had been backing Allen up on the streets of Kandahar, the good-tempered soldier being something of a protégé of Allen's.

'Chocka full of girls, it is.' The Welshman grinned.

The sergeant major overheard the excitement and started to laugh along with Allen.

Bagram Airbase, a former Soviet airfield, was now the US military's largest base in Afghanistan. Located about 60km north of Kabul, it was the home of NATO's HQ, along with their country's fortress-like embassies. During the invasion the base was secured by the Special Boat Service and then used for a while by the Royal Marines before it was handed over to the US. The runways had been extended to accommodate the heavy-lift and attack aircraft based there. The base was vast, covering nearly 80 square kilometres, and had the atmosphere of a Wild West boom town. But unlike Dodge City this town was an alcohol-free zone. This whole war was. It hadn't always been like that. At one time, NATO headquarters in Afghanistan had had at least seven bars that served tax-free beer and wine, including a sport bar named Tora Bora. Then, in 2009 General Stanley McChrystal, Commander of NATO forces in Afghanistan, tried to contact his HQ and find out information about the deaths of 125 civilians during some air strikes. Finding that the troops were unable to respond adequately to the incident because they were alleged to be drunk, he imposed a blanket ban – including to foreign troops. Despite prohibition, alcohol could still be found at the bases, smuggled in by foreign dealers or posted by family and friends hidden in other items.

However, the thousands of personnel housed there wanted for nothing. From its own hospital and support facilities, and everything from coffee shops and Häagen-Dazs ice cream parlours to bowling alleys, it was Little America, a home from home.

But Taff wasn't going to experience any of the fun stuff.

The American special ops command was based at Bagram and had their own fenced-off compounds within the base which were secure areas within an already secure airbase. Operations dictate that once a warning order is given, the operators involved and their support staff go into isolation while they plan and prepare. Operational Security is paramount. Only the people who need to know will get to know. Op Sec ensures there are no leaks. Of course there were other secure areas where insurgents were held for interrogation by people like Vasquez and Powell.

But no one ever spoke about what was going on in those 'facilities'.

CHAPTER 16

BADAKHSHAN PROVINCE

Laura Jones had never felt so scared in her life.

When the bandits had first appeared around them it hadn't felt real. It was a dream, a bad dream, as if it was happening to someone else. She'd been shocked into silence, too terrified to scream. She couldn't have run if she'd tried. In the initial moments of capture, Laura had discovered what it truly meant to be petrified: she had been terrified into total stillness.

The men who had captured them had roguish smiles and laughed with each other, seemingly delighted with their prize. Laura had expected the worst, and she had almost cried with relief when she wasn't pulled from her mule and raped. It was still a terrible fear in her mind, but so far the kidnappers had treated her and the other women with dignity: at least, as much dignity as it was possible to have when another human being has enslaved you. It was a low bar that she prayed would not sink lower.

'Everything will be all right,' Tasneem told Laura as their mules were pushed close together in a narrow mountain pass. 'If they wanted to hurt us they would have done it already.'

'If they don't want to hurt us then why are they armed?'

'Everyone is armed here. It's a dangerous place.'

'We weren't armed,' Laura replied, feeling foolish. 'We should have had guards.'

'We have God,' Tasneem said, as though that settled the matter. She was the most religious of the four women. Laura had never considered herself a religious person, but she'd prayed more in the past few hours than she had done in the three decades of her life.

'Who are they, do you think?' she asked her Afghan friend.

'Their accents are from Badakhshan. I think they're just bandits, Laura.'

'*Just* bandits?' Laura asked. Tasneem made it sound so harmless.

'They're not Taliban, or worse, at least.'

'What will they do with us?'

'That,' Tasneem said, 'we shall have to wait to find out. Until then, drink when you can, eat when you can, and sleep when you can. When the time comes, we must be ready.'

CHAPTER 17

Umid watched the pair of hostages talk, but didn't tell them to be silent. Sherali didn't seem to mind, and if it was okay by him, then it was okay by Umid.

The young man's feet were sore but his heart was happy and his head was full of dreams. They were the dreams of many 18-year-old men: dreams of money, of success, of a wife. Umid thought that he could have it all. The four aid workers had been taken without a fight and barely a whisper, and Sherali had promised him that when their ransom was paid, every man in the group would receive a substantial part of the prize. The old bandit was vague on numbers, but he promised Umid that it would be enough to set him up as a man. A real man, with property and potential. The kind of man who could start a family and be proud of what he had done.

Despite his profession, and his craggy looks, Umid reckoned that Sherali was a kind man. After all, he was allowing the captives to ride their mules, led by the reins by bandits and with their hands bound together. It didn't occur to Umid that the bandit did so because he didn't want one of them to die or injure themselves on the hard paths through the mountains, and ruin his chances of ransoming them back to their organisation or nation.

Umid walked at the back of the group; he studied the four hostages. Two of them were Afghan. They spoke Dari, though they had uttered very few words except to accept their position and promise that they would not attempt to escape. One hostage was African and another was from Britain. Her people were an enemy to the Taliban, and in the past, when they were an empire, they were the enemies of Afghanistan. Still, the British were hated less than the Americans. Umid's fellow bandits blamed them for the current war. The men who had flown planes into America's towers were Saudis, but America had chosen to make Saudi Arabia its ally, and launched a war on Afghanistan instead. It made no sense unless America planned on making Afghanistan a part of an empire, as Britain and Russia had tried and failed to do.

'This war will be no different,' Sherali told Umid as they hiked through the mountain passes of their homeland. 'We will drive this enemy out as we have all others.'

'You will fight for the Taliban?' Umid had asked him, but the old mujahid had laughed.

'My fighting days are over, Umid. Now I want to be rich. Let young men fight the wars.'

Umid had thought on Sherali's words: should he join the Taliban himself and drive out the invader? No answer came easily to him. His father had fought the Soviets, but one of his oldest cousins had died fighting for the Northern Alliance against the Taliban. They were dominated by Pashtos, who were as alien to Umid as the British. As much as he hated America for bringing their bombs to his country, he found no love for the Taliban in his heart. He had found a place here, instead. Working with men of his own sect. Let the Taliban and Americans fight their war. Umid would follow in the steps of generations of men from the northeast of Afghanistan, and fight for himself.

After a day of hard walking through the wooded valleys, they sheltered for the night in the ruins of a small village, nothing left of the homes but mudbrick walls. The mules were tethered, and the hostages put under guard in a ruined dwelling. Umid collected firewood, then watched as Sherali tended to the flames.

'Ever see a place like this?' the old bandit asked him.

Umid shook his head. 'No. I've never left Fayzabad.'

'There are villages like this all over Afghanistan,' the older man told him.

'How did you know it was here?'

'I know these mountains as well as I do my own hands,' Sherali told him, throwing another branch onto the fire. 'It was the Russians,' Sherali said, his eyes on the flames. 'They surrounded this village, rounded up everyone who lived here, then slaughtered them like cattle. Women, old men, children. Not one was left alive.'

'How do you know this?' Umid asked after a moment.

Sherali turned to face him. 'Because we're sitting in my home.'

Umid didn't know what to say. The old bandit turned back to the fire.

'I was your age at the time, away and fighting jihad against the Russians. The war was over before I came back here and found my family.'

'I'm sorry.'

'Why? They are in paradise, Umid. I hope that I have done enough in God's eyes that one day I will join them.'

For a long moment he said nothing. 'Go to Daler,' he said at last. 'He's with the women. Tell him to bring them here.'

Umid did as he was told. Daler was in his late twenties, with skin ravaged and pockmarked by childhood disease.

'Sherali wants you to bring the women to him.'

Daler ordered the captives onto their feet. Umid watched their expressions. Their eyes were so haunted that they were almost vacant. Did they expect to be raped? Tortured? Umid knew that such things happened in war, but Sherali had seemed so calm by the fire. Surely it was not that.

'You lead the way,' Daler told him. 'I'll bring up the rear. Watch them, Umid. They look like women, but they are snakes. You can't trust them, you understand? Not even for a moment.'

Umid nodded and led on. When they were inside the walls of what had once been Sherali's home, the bandits' leader pushed the captives down onto their knees beside the fire, then pulled a phone from his pocket.

Umid's stomach lurched. His cousin had shown him a video that featured beheadings by a Taliban leader and, for a moment, Umid felt bile rise in his throat and his legs weakened. He'd never watched a human die, let alone see one beheaded. He only prayed that he would not be asked to kill them himself.

'Say your names,' Sherali told the captives. The two Afghans spoke first, then the foreigners.

Umid felt light-headed.

'You look as white as her,' Daler whispered to him. 'Are you sick?'

'Just nervous.'

'You think we're going to kill them?' Daler laughed. 'You don't get paid for dead hostages, Umid. This is a ransom video. To show who we have, and that they are still alive. There's no profit in bodies. Not for us.'

Relief flooded through the young man. 'So they will live?'

'For now, yes.' The bandit shrugged. 'For how long depends on the answers of their governments.'

CHAPTER 18

KABUL

Rachael Powell sat waiting for the satlink with Number 10 to come to life. She was in 'the basement', an airless room in the British Embassy that served as a secure comms centre. To her right sat the UK's oversight group for the operation: a British general, and beside him the UK's ambassador to Afghanistan. The general was the second highest ranking member of the NATO force in the country, and a former director of UK Special Forces (UKSF). He was 2i/c, second in command, to the US Commander NATO Forces Afghanistan. The two men had an excellent relationship. Both of them supported the approach of using special operations forces wherever possible to target the Taliban's commanders, bomb makers, logisticians and money men.

Powell had only met the ambassador on a few occasions. Her role was to advise and assist Britain's military mission rather than its political and economic aims. But with two messy divorces in 12 years, one an army officer, the other a member of the House of Lords with a ministerial position at the Home Office, she knew how blurred the lines were between the two.

The wide screen in front of them blinked to life, and Powell saw a new face representing the prime minister sitting in front of the camera. He might be new, but the 'link room' wall was still the same stark and naked brilliant white behind him.

This man was older than the last one, maybe in his mid-fifties, but with all the makings of a bureaucrat. Sensible haircut, sensible suit, shirt and tie. They might look boring, but these people really do run the country.

The bureaucrat greeted the two men beside Powell before she was acknowledged. That was fine by her; there was a pecking order and the ambassador was number one. She wasn't in the country to play politics; she was there because it seemed like the best way that she could contribute to killing terrorists, and anyone else that threatened the lives of her countrymen. Powell's father had served most of his adult life in the Royal Navy, which meant that her mother had spent most of hers at the whim of the service too, moving wherever her husband was ordered. Both of Powell's grandfathers had fought against the Nazis, and their fathers in the trenches. It was a fiercely patriotic family to which Rachael Powell felt honoured to belong. Even her brother was a soldier, and that was how she met her first husband. But now her brother was dead, killed by insurgents in Iraq. That was her biggest motivation.

'Thank you all for coming.' The bureaucrat gave a smile that seemed genuine. 'Let's get started, shall we? General?'

The man seated beside Powell began. 'Two hours ago, the Afghan government received a ransom demand for four aid workers that have been kidnapped in Badakhshan Province. Two are Afghan nationals, one is Kenyan, and another is British. Our intelligence has confirmed their identities, and corroborated the video that they sent as proof of life. It was taken' – he checked his notes and wristwatch – '14 hours ago. At that time, they all appeared alive and unharmed.'

'Well that's good news, at least. Tell me more about ... Badakhshan, was it?'

The general deferred to the person who knew more. 'I believe Powell is best placed to answer that.'

'And Powell,' the bureaucrat asked, 'you're with ...'

'She's with intelligence, sir,' the general answered for her.

'Ah,' said the bureaucrat, recognising that some things were best left unsaid. 'Please go on, Mrs Powell.'

'It's Miss,' she corrected him, not because she was insulted but because in her world, where details were usually a matter of life and death, a person's accuracy was how they were measured. 'Badakhshan is a frontier province in the northeast of the country. It borders Tajikistan, China and Pakistan, making it a key area for smugglers. The terrain lends itself to this work. Badakhshan is mountainous, with the mountains often covered in forest. The population is predominantly Tajik, and around one million people. The province's population centres have fewer than 100,000 residents, with most under 50,000.

'The people of Badakhshan have a history of resisting the Taliban. It was the only province that did not fall to the Taliban during the civil war. Until 2010 there was very little Taliban activity there, but this has increased in recent years. That being said, it is not a safe place. Drug smuggling is controlled by warlords, and banditry is common. There are large mineral deposits there, but it is one of the poorest areas in the world.'

'That makes for desperate people.'

Powell was warming towards the bureaucrat. It was clear to her that he was assimilating every word she said. That was important, because he would not be the one to give the go/no-go for a hostage rescue. The prime minister would. But since the failure of the last rescue attempt in the Korengal and the political currency lost in the UK, the PM had adopted a hands-off approach to special forces (SF) operations. It was this faceless bureaucrat who held the keys to unlock any rescue operation.

'Yes, exactly. Sixty per cent of Badakhshan's population live below the national poverty line, which, as you can imagine, is a very low line to begin with.'

'Hmm. And the kidnappers?'

Powell looked to the general beside her, expecting him to answer. Instead he gestured that she should do so.

'Yes. From the ransom demand delivered to the Afghan government, it appears that this is not an incident connected to the Taliban or any ideology. It's about cash.'

The bureaucrat leaned back in his chair. 'How much?'

'Seven million US dollars,' the British ambassador replied. 'And the release of one of their own.'

'Who?'

'A drug smuggler. He's locked up in Bagram.'

'And what have the Afghan government said?'

'They're happy for NATO to proceed how we see fit.'

'Good. So what are our options?'

'We have three,' the general beside Powell replied. 'One, we accept the deal, pay the ransom and release their man.'

The bureaucrat shook his head, yet was still smiling. 'Britain does not negotiate with terrorists.'

'There's nothing to suggest they're terrorists.'

The bureaucrat shook his head once more. 'They kidnapped a British citizen. That makes them terrorists. The country will not accept any other classification. Situations like this have to be presented in a black or white format, no grey. So, option two?'

'We ask the Afghan government to handle it,' the ambassador replied. It wasn't a serious proposition, and everyone knew it. The Afghan government and military were allies, but they were junior partners, and less capable than Western militaries. It wouldn't just be the hostages' lives on the line if the job was given to the Afghans and they failed: there would be more political currency lost for not even trying to rescue the hostages.

'And the final option?' he asked.

'We handle it ourselves,' the general said. 'With special forces.'

The bureaucrat leaned forward in his chair, his face now almost filling the screen.

'I will speak with the prime minister. I'm sure you will be preparing for a go, and that should continue. Thank you all for your time.'

CHAPTER 19

BAGRAM

An hour after Powell had turned off the satlink in Kabul, Allen and the other SAS operators that had flown from Kandahar were sitting in a briefing room.

'Any idea what this job's about?' Taff asked.

'You know as much as I do.'

One of the squadron's officers walked to the front of the room. Far from the stereotypical public school 'Rupert' of film and TV, Sean Coates had grown up in a working-class town in North Yorkshire. The army had changed a lot since the nineties when it came to its officer selection. Over 50 per cent of Sandhurst cadets now came from state schools and hadn't had a university education. After his A-levels Coates had applied to Sandhurst, and had been one of the few from his intake to be accepted into the Parachute Regiment, before going on and passing special forces selection. Coates had a reputation as a good boxer, and the broken nose to go with it. Allen considered him a well-measured and competent leader of men.

'All right, listen in. Situation: Four aid workers have been taken hostage in Badakhshan Province. We are here to spin up and be prepared to effect a rescue. So far all we've got are names, so we could be waiting a while. You know how long these things can take to put together. Plus, we will need the go or no-go from London.'

Allen knew it well. It had been two weeks between the hostage being kidnapped and the failed attempt at rescue in the Korengal. There were no certainties on timelines, but Allen was sure of one thing: if this job happened, Allen would make sure he didn't have to experience another innocent and caring woman die in his arms.

'While we wait for the spooks to build the intelligence picture we're going to get up to speed on our hostage rescue skills,' the officer went on. 'We've been kicking in doors for months, so this will be a little different. The priority is saving a life, not shooting some fucker in the face.'

'Do we know who took them, boss?' a corporal asked.

'Not specifically, but it's not Taliban or Al-Qaeda. So it's a good possibility it's bandits after a ransom, but that doesn't mean the Taliban or AQ won't get involved. They've got their own intelligence networks and it won't be long before they get wind of these four, and there's nothing to say they won't try and get to them before us, and then we have more online beheadings. Any more questions?'

There were none. Until the intelligence picture was built, there was little for the soldiers to do but get prepped up as best they could and stand by.

As the operators started to leave the room Taff closed in on Allen, smiling. 'This is my first one, you know, a big job with the lads,' he said, but Allen shared none of his enthusiasm.

'Yep, a big one, but it won't only be us, Taff. Just watch.'

CHAPTER 20

Not far away from the briefing room where the SAS had finally been told why they had been flown north to Bagram, Rachael Powell met Vasquez in a CIA operations room inside their own secured 'facility'.

'How'd your meeting go?' the American asked her, offering a cigarette.

Powell took it, having never had the guilt trip of the nicotine hit when smoking with her friend. 'I corrected the new "guy",' she said with a smile, 'so my next posting will probably be to the Falklands.'

'I've heard they have penguins,' Vasquez said as he lit them both up. He liked it when they were together; it made him feel he was just being polite by smoking with her. 'A few things happened while you were away. You want the good news or bad news first?'

'Bad.'

'Our analysts haven't been able to pull much from the video. As you know, we were able to pull the data to show that it was taken last night, but the quality means the cell is cheap or old. But anyhow, we haven't been able to pick up much background. We think two other men are talking in the background, but we haven't been able to make out what they're saying.'

'At least that tells us there's at least three of them,' Powell said. 'The two talking, and whoever took the video.'

'Sure,' Vasquez allowed. 'But we wouldn't expect less than that if they were taking four hostages. My guess would be there's at least six. Two to watch the hostages, two to act as lookouts and two resting.'

Powell nodded. 'That would make sense. And the good news?'

The American smiled. 'We weren't able to pull a location off the video's data, but we've triangulated the signal of the cell used to make the demand. I've put in a request to get a drone to check the area out. Should be getting the go-ahead anytime now.'

CHAPTER 21

CREECH AIR FORCE BASE, NEVADA, USA

Captain Sarah Cohen sat back in her chair and flexed the fingers on her right hand around a joystick. She wore green flight overalls but no helmet, the cockpit of her aircraft very different from those that her father had flown in Vietnam. In front of Cohen was a bank of screens showing systems information and camera footage that was coming to her from the other side of the world. Cohen was a drone pilot, and her Predator was about to take off in Afghanistan on a highest priority mission.

'I have control,' she said into her headset, letting the ground staff in Bagram know that their part in the operation was over, for now.

Powered by propellers at the rear of its fuselage, the Predator climbed into a blue sky. Drones were changing the face of aerial warfare; they could be piloted from United States soil while striking targets in Afghanistan, Pakistan and other countries. The drone programme was loved by American leaders, but hated by many others, who claimed that it often violated international law, and even American law.

Because of controversies around the programme, Cohen was often reluctant to tell people what she did for a living, particularly when she was relaxing in the nearby city of Las Vegas. She preferred to hang around people from work, who understood the complexities of her position. Cohen was responsible for the deaths of several terrorists, but they had come at the price of 'collateral damage'. Cohen told herself that it was a necessary evil to protect America and its service people overseas. She couldn't let doubt enter her mind.

Not everyone was able to handle the pressure, and the questions, like Cohen could. She knew drone operators from her Attack Squadron who'd had to leave the job for psychological reasons. A couple of others had moral objections. She didn't think less of them because of it. They had their reasons, and she had hers.

The Predator drones were a mainstay of the War on Terror, used for surveillance, targets acquisition and strikes. The Predator had an endurance of 40 hours and could deliver real-time imagery via satellite from its range of cameras, laser designators and multi-mode all-weather radar. On top of that, it was also the first-ever armed unmanned aerial vehicle capable of firing an air-to-ground weapon. Its Hellfire missiles could carry a variety of warheads, including high explosive, and shaped charges for anti-armour attacks – but Cohen would not be attacking any targets today. To lighten the load on the drone, and increase the time that it could stay up in the sky, her Predator was flying without armament. Cohen's mission was to survey an area in Badakhshan Province. She didn't know why, and that was often how it worked: 'need to know'. Her job was to get the aircraft in position and keep it there. It would be up to the intelligence analysts to decipher what the cameras were seeing.

The Predator cruised at a speed of 90mph. Compared to the other aircraft in the sky it was slow, very slow, but

Cohen didn't mind. Afghanistan was a beautiful country, and she enjoyed seeing it through the Predator's sensors. The mountains reminded her of the ones around Las Vegas: steep, barren and forbidding.

'How are we looking?' Cohen asked her systems weapons operator.

'All good,' Ben Kerallis replied. 'How long until we're on target?'

'Another three hours.'

'Well, there's not much for me to do until then. I'm gonna go take a leak and grab us some coffee.'

Remote piloting had its perks. Cohen's father was always ribbing her that she was able to drink coffee on a mission.

'What did you use to stay alert?' she'd asked him once.

'The enemy,' he'd replied, laughing.

His war had been very different to hers, with the ever-present threat of anti-aircraft fire, surface-to-air missiles, and even enemy fighters. Those weren't concerns for the Predators over Afghanistan. The enemy had no aircraft of their own and the Predator's altitude put it well out of the way of any ground fire. The drones could operate and strike with impunity. He'd never said it to her, but Cohen reckoned that her father looked down on that. He was still of the dogfighting generation, with its ingrained sense of fair play. Man on man. Pilot against pilot. Cohen understood the sentiment but she didn't agree with it. To her, the only thing that mattered was winning. The bigger advantage that America had, the better.

Stronger than expected headwinds meant that it took three and a half hours for the Predator to reach the target area it had been assigned to cover. Kerallis talked about his children, who were in school a 20-minute drive from where they were operating the drone. It was Kerallis's job to operate the Predator's weaponry. There had been times where he had killed people and been home playing with his children a few hours later. He thought of himself more similar to a police officer fighting inside the war battlespace. The mindset meant he went to work and did his job, and then he would get back into the real world by cutting the grass and petting the cat. Kerallis had found a way to compartmentalise his war on a daily basis.

'On target,' she told Kerallis.

Cohen sipped some coffee from a cup emblazoned with her squadron's logo, then put the aircraft into a gentle turn, a pattern she would hold as the Predator circled the ground like a vulture. Cohen kept the aircraft at a height of 20,000 feet, where it would be a speck in the sky to those on the ground. The Predator's engine and propellers were far quieter than the fast jets that ripped and roared through Afghanistan's skies.

The Predator's pilot watched the screens. In another part of the United States, analysts were watching the drone's footage. What they were looking for exactly, Cohen didn't know. The area that the drone was circling above looked empty of human life. The mountains were steep, many of the slopes cloaked in forest.

'That looks like a track, don't you think?' Kerallis said to her.

'Maybe. A footpath. Maybe.'

It was hard to picture vehicles getting in and out of the place. It was as desolate as it got.

'I'm going to switch the camera to thermal,' Kerallis said, and one of the screens blinked back to life in blacks and whites.

A white-hot shape of a bird flashed low across the forest. For a half-hour more there were no signs of life.

'There,' Cohen said suddenly. 'What was that?'

'Another bird?'

'I don't know. It looked small, but – look, there it is again! What is that?'

Something the size of a soccer ball had appeared on the side of one of the mountains. It was there for a moment, and then disappeared.

'Weird,' Kerallis uttered.

Cohen said nothing. She'd seen something like this before. She took her aircraft around in a wide arc. 'Put the high-res cameras where we saw the thermal signature.'

'Roger.'

Cohen dropped a few thousand feet of altitude, and brought the aircraft level with where the signature had been seen.

'Well I'll be damned...' Kerallis said. 'A cave.'

'Someone was putting their head out to look around.' Cohen smiled. 'Whatever we were looking for, I think we just found it.'

CHAPTER 22

BAGRAM

Some called it Afghanistan's Guantanamo Bay. Others, the Black Dungeon. Whatever the name, it was clear to Rachael Powell when she started her tour that spending time in the CIA-run detention centre at Bagram would be no picnic. The place was cramped, loud, and stank of body odour, sweat and worse.

Powell walked with Vasquez along a dingy corridor. They were here to see the man that the hostage-takers wanted released.

'The scumbag's name is Jallah,' the CIA man told her. 'He got picked up in an anti-narcotics operation last year.'

'Any connections to the Taliban or AQ?'

'No one runs drugs without both of them having a hand in it.'

'Any prior kidnappings by any associates?'

'That we know of, no, but that just means no Westerners were involved.'

Powell said nothing, but nodded. It was a sad reality that most of the country's events went unnoticed by the West unless it involved their own citizens. There wasn't anything Powell could do about that. It was just the way it was. A child killed by a drunk driver in Birmingham would create national headlines, but 16 kids killed by Brits during a bombing raid there, who cares?

'What do you expect to get out of him?' Powell asked.

'Honestly, nothing,' the American confessed, 'but I want to look him in the eye, and see who it is they want. Maybe, when I give him the news, he'll let something slip, but a lot of these fuckers have a code of honour. They're happy to throw other tribes and sects under the bus, but with their own most of them would rather die than talk.'

Vasquez stopped next to a closed door. 'Ready?' he asked her.

'Let's do it.'

Vasquez put on a mean dog face and opened the door. Powell followed behind him. There was a single chair in the interrogation room. It was bolted to the floor, and the man in the chair had his hands bound behind him. He was an ugly man and the way he looked at Powell was uglier still.

Powell looked away, not in fear but as though she was bored. She cast her eyes around at the surroundings that she knew so well. There were new bloodstains on the floor. They had to be recent, because the interrogation rooms were regularly hosed down.

'Jallah,' Vasquez said, 'a few of your friends have made a mistake. A big mistake.' He spoke in Dari. Like Powell, the intelligence man was an excellent linguist, but the Afghan said nothing in reply.

'Four aid workers have been kidnapped in Badakhshan. Part of the ransom includes your release.'

Jallah smiled, but said nothing.

'I'm sure you know how these things end,' Vasquez said casually. 'We say no to the demands, we find them, and then we shoot them in the fucking face and leave your friends' bodies for the dogs. Is that what you want for your friends, and maybe you? Or perhaps you'd like to talk some sense into them, and tell them to let the hostages go?'

'They are not cowards,' the Afghan replied. 'If you think you can find them, and kill them, then try it. That worked well for you in Kunar, didn't it?'

Powell watched Vasquez's reaction. She wasn't surprised that the bandit would know about SEAL Team Six's failed raid. It had been international news, and a cause of celebration for anyone who hated the Americans.

'You seem happy,' Vasquez told the Afghan.

'Of course.' The bandit looked him in the eye. 'Why wouldn't I be? God willing, I will soon be a free man. Have you ever spent a night here yourself, American?'

'Only criminals go to jail, buddy.'

Jallah sneered. 'Americans are the biggest criminals. The world's gangsters. That is why you can treat people like this. We hardly eat. We live like animals, one bucket between 40 men to shit in. Tell me, where is your human rights here?'

'You need to be human to have human rights,' Vasquez told him.

'*You* would say that? An American? The crime of which I am accused is smuggling. Do you treat your pilots like this? The ones who have killed thousands and thousands of this country's women and children? If I am not human, what does that make you?'

'The winners,' Vasquez said with a smile.

The Afghan was not impressed. 'You may be winning at the moment, but that does not mean that you will be the winners.'

'Put it in a book, Jallah. You've got the time. All the time in the world, in fact.'

'The only book I need is the Qur'an.'

'Really? I didn't think a smuggler would be a religious man.'

'I am a prisoner, not a smuggler, and a prisoner requires faith more than he does food and water, which is good, because America does not appear so fond of feeding its prisoners.'

'You're not an American prisoner, Jallah. You belong to the Afghan government.'

'And yet here I am, talking to an American, in a prison run by Americans. I know how your country works. You think by exporting your torture sites it absolves you of blame. Do your citizens truly believe that you are just, or do you lie to them as much as you lie to yourselves?'

Jallah didn't get a chance to say another word, the back of Vasquez's hand shutting his mouth closed. 'Philosophy class is over, you piece of shit. Let me tell you, Jallah, I've got no confusion about who I am, or what I'm willing to do to get information out of you. You think sharing a toilet with 40 other people's bad? Wait until I lock you up in the fucking sewer.'

'Do that, American, and my men will make the hostages into even greater whores than your mother was.'

Vasquez hit him once, twice, three times. Jallah's head was reeling, and blood trickled from the corners of his mouth, but he was smiling.

Powell took Vasquez by the arm. 'Let's go,' she said. But the American wouldn't take his eyes off Jallah.

'Hey,' Powell said into his ear. 'Let's go. Leave him be. He's just a smuggler, for fuck's sake.'

The CIA agent stared at the bandit for a moment longer, then gave a single, short nod.

'If your men touch so much as a hair on the hostages' heads,' he told Jallah, 'I'll take yours from your shoulders. That's a promise. That's a goddamn fucking promise.'

Powell and Vasquez didn't speak as they returned to the operations centre. Not because either had an issue with what had occurred in the interrogation room, but because they had analytical minds, and were replaying Jallah's words, and filing them away in the complex web that was intelligence work in Afghanistan. Each had played their part perfectly in the interrogation room. They'd had enough practice. Now wasn't the time to start gripping Jallah, because the interrogation would contain so many questions. If they didn't get the intelligence they needed elsewhere, then both of them would be gripping Jallah big-time for the final details.

When they entered their ops room, one of Vasquez's team almost ran over to him.

'What is it?' Vasquez asked the smiling man.

'It's the hostages! We think we've found them!'

CHAPTER 23

BADAKHSHAN PROVINCE

Umid wandered the cave, his head filled with thoughts of the brave mujahideen who had fought against the Russians in these hills and valleys. Something caught the beam of his torchlight. It was half-buried, but unmistakeable. Umid dropped to one knee and retrieved it from the dirt. It was a 7.62mm 'short' – the same round as the ones in the magazine of his rifle, but to Umid this was special: a relic of his father who had fought here when he was Umid's age.

He unloaded his AK, cleaned off the round and pushed it into his magazine before reloading. He had never felt so close to his father as this moment.

The smell of something hit Umid's nostrils and he was instantly hungry. He traced his steps back through the winding caves. Close to the cave mouth, Daler was cooking a pot of meat over the flames. The smoke of the fire stung Umid's eyes, but Sherali had ordered that there were to be no fires outside. In fact, he had ordered that no one was to leave the caves, not even to relieve themselves.

'You never know where the Americans are watching,' he had told his men. 'There is enough room in here for an army. Until we get word that the ransom has been paid, and Jallah is released, we will stay here.'

Three of the mules were released. An unlucky fourth was slaughtered and some of it turned into stew.

'It's good,' Umid said as he ate his portion. Growing up in poverty he had come to appreciate a full belly.

Umid sat and ate with the other bandits. Two men were watching the women, who had been put into one of the cave's chambers, and two more stood watch at the tunnel mouth. There was no chance for the hostages to escape. The cave had just one way in and the same way out, not like so many of the caves that had been rejected. Sherali had picked this place well, and Umid was impressed.

He listened as the bandits told jokes and stories. Some talked about their families, while others had no family to speak of. What they all had in common was their desire to be richer than they were today.

When Sherali spoke every man listened. He spoke about hundreds of caves that had been dug into these mountains for thousands of years to defend the people from the country's invaders. Darius I of Babylonia, Alexander the Great, Genghis Khan, the British, the Russians, and now the Americans – along with the British once again. Sometimes the younger men could convince him to tell tales of jihad against the Russians when he fought them from these very hills. Using the cave systems to hide from Russian artillery, moving along the tunnels that were dug deep into the hillsides to appear from behind the invaders and destroy them. These he delivered sometimes with a smile. When he spoke of fallen brothers, it was with pride. They were martyrs, and in paradise. Of course, Sherali missed their company, but a part of him envied their fates. It was a beautiful thing to die in war against an infidel.

'Should we be fighting for the Taliban?' one of the men asked their leader. 'The Americans are infidels.'

'They are,' Sherali agreed, 'but most of the men facing the Taliban are not. The men of the Afghan Army are fellow Muslims, and many of them are from the north. I trust the Taliban more than I trust the Americans, but that does not mean I think they are righteous. Look what they did to the Lion of Panjshir. He was a great leader, a great Afghan, and they allowed Al-Qaeda to murder him. There was no honour in it. It is one thing to die in battle, but suicide attacks? They are cowardly.'

'They say that the men who die in such attacks are martyred and go to paradise, Sherali. Do you not agree?'

'I don't know. Allah is merciful. More merciful than any man. But would he reward someone who killed dozens of believers? Women and children? You've heard of what they do in Iraq. That, to me, is not jihad. That is not martyrdom.'

'I have a cousin in the Taliban,' one of the bandits said. 'I am very proud of him.'

A few of the other men shared similar stories.

'My cousin is fighting, too,' Daler spoke up. 'He is with the government's forces, and I can say with an honest heart that he is a good Muslim, and a good Afghan. I agree with Sherali. This war, it is too messy. Too confusing. If I thought there was a clear side to join then I would do so, without hesitation, but I don't. Instead I will provide for my family.'

'You will provide for them well when we receive the ransom.' Sherali smiled. 'I have been promised that each one of us will be rewarded, and handsomely. You have my word on this.' Sherali ate another mouthful. 'The stew is excellent, Daler. Umid, have you finished eating? Fill up that big bowl there. Take some spoons, and take it to the women. Make sure you get all of the spoons back.'

Something in Sherali's tone told him that the old bandit had first-hand experience of someone, maybe himself, using a spoon for a weapon. Umid did as he was told, and tried not to imagine having his eyes plucked from his skull.

Further inside, the caverns were lit by lights run from a diesel generator that chugged away deeper in one of the cave's chambers. Sherali had told his men to stay clear of it, as the fumes would go to a man's head. 'We must keep all the heat inside the caves,' he had told the bandits. 'The Americans can see it.'

Umid thought that such precaution was prudent. Their homeland was a maze of mountains and forests, but it wasn't unusual to see American aircraft in the skies, and everyone knew that it was the most technologically advanced country in the world. If Sherali said that the Americans could see heat, then Umid believed him. The old bandit had lived this long for a reason.

The young Afghan nodded a greeting to the two men guarding the hostages' chamber and went inside with their food. The four women were huddled together, and silent. The lights inside the caves were weak, but Umid could see enough to know that they were scared.

'Here,' he said, placing the deep bowl of stew in front of them. 'It's good.'

The English woman looked at it, then said something to one of the Afghan women that Umid did not understand.

'What is the meat?' she asked Umid.

'Mule.'

'What is your name?' the oldest woman asked.

'Umid.'

'My name is Tasneem. How old are you, Umid?'

'Eighteen.'

'Do you have brothers? Sisters?'

'I do.'

'Do they all live?'

'No. Two ... they died ...'

Tasneem looked pained. 'I'm sorry, Umid. I know it is a difficult thing.'

Umid said nothing.

'I am trying to do God's work, Umid. To show his mercy, by ending the deaths of children.'

Umid said nothing, but nodded. What the woman was saying made sense to him.

'We are not bad people, Umid.'

The young man was about to reply, but didn't get the chance. One of the guards walked by him and kicked the bowl over, the stew sloshing out across the floor. 'If you were hungry you'd be eating, not talking,' he scolded Tasneem, then turned to Umid.

'Next time, let them eat with their hands.'

Umid collected the bowl, and the spoons.

Before he left the room, he looked back at Tasneem. He spoke no words, but his eyes said *sorry*.

CHAPTER 24

BAGRAM

After a day of training, working through the hostage rescue drills for which the SAS was famous, Allen and the other men had been called back to the briefing room to receive an update on the situation. When he saw who was already waiting inside, Allen stopped in the doorway and turned to Taff.

'I fucking told you so.'

Seated inside were Alex Banks and a team of SEALs.

Allen locked his eyes on to Banks. 'Can't get rid of you, can I?'

It raised a smile from Banks but there wasn't time for any catch-up as Coates entered and walked to the front of the room. 'Gentlemen.' There were two strangers with him. One was a bald Latino. The other was a taller woman with a no-nonsense air. She was the only woman in a room full of men – violent men – but if she was bothered by that, then she didn't show a bit of it. It was the kind of attitude that Allen admired, and he quickly decided that he liked her.

'So,' Coates began. 'This is Federico Vasquez and Rachael Powell. They're going to give us an update on the situation.'

Allen smiled to himself. Coates might as well have made air quotes when he said their names. The operators were used to having contact with these people. In the 'dirty war', intelligence and special forces were two knuckles on the same fist, and both SEALs and SAS could sniff them a mile away. What they were called meant nothing to anyone because there was a high possibility they weren't their real names anyway.

It was 'Powell' who spoke first. 'As you are aware, four aid workers have been kidnapped in Badakhshan Province. The four women work for a medical NGO who reported them missing and has since corroborated their identities.' Powell went on to list their names. Her accent gave Allen an idea where she fitted into all this: she was Secret Intelligence Service (SIS).

'Two of the women are Afghan, one is Kenyan and one is a UK national. Both the Afghan and Kenyan governments have requested NATO help in recovering their citizens. Due to the nationality of the fourth hostage, this is to be a UK-led operation, but a joint one. The Commander NATO Forces wants this operation conducted jointly by UKSF and DEVGRU.'

Allen tried to keep the disappointment from his face. This was a mission that he and his squadron mates could handle alone, he was certain of it, but he wasn't surprised that it was being handled this way.

'Earlier today,' the intelligence service agent went on, 'US command dispatched a drone to look at an area where we believe the ransom demand was made, and so a high possibility that the hostages were still in the area.'

Powell clicked a device in her hand and a wide screen relayed footage of a mountainous area. Allen watched as the camera zoomed in.

'Note the cave entrance and the movement of one body, unidentified.'

The imagery on the screen changed.

'What you're looking at is three mules, with no riders. We believe these are the mules that the hostages were using.

Allen kept looking at the camera feed. 'Are those vehicle tracks?'

The woman looked at her counterpart. 'Our analysts think so,' Vasquez replied. 'They can't determine how old they are, but they're positive there were three.'

'So there could be up to 40 men in that cave with the women.' Allen now knew the bald man was CIA and decided he liked him too.

'There could be, yes.'

'The good news,' Powell continued, 'is that from the ransom video the hostages appear unharmed.'

'What's the ransom?' someone asked from the back of the room. Allen recognised the voice as Miller's, and once Powell found the face that asked in the crowd she replied.

'Seven million US and the release of a prisoner. Which is not going to happen.'

'We now have continuous surveillance from Predators,' Vasquez said. 'There has been no more movement outside of the cave or surrounding area.

'But these mountains are honeycombed with cave systems. They have been constantly excavated by the local population since 500BC. During the Russian invasion, this area became a mujahideen stronghold, and they dug tunnels through the rock to connect the caves. We have no idea if our cave is internally connected to a tunnel and so connected to other caves in the area, and therefore a means of movement or escape without us being aware.

'There's a slight heat signature at the cave mouth, probably from a fire, or fuel heating maybe. So, until we learn more, there is a medium possibility that whoever we have in that mountainside is still in this cave.'

'Or the body heat off 40 men,' Allen said.

The CIA agent nodded. 'That's possible,' he conceded. 'Any other thoughts?'

Allen had a big one. 'So we know there is a body, or maybe bodies, in the cave, but we don't know if the hostages are there.'

'Correct.'

'Do the takers normally keep moving them to different locations for security? If they're in the cave could we hit them in transit?'

Fighting in a cave is much more dangerous for everyone involved. Out in the open is far more efficient. But it wasn't just a tactical question. What Allen was thinking about was the prospect of four more of these crazy women that he so admired being killed during an op. He didn't want those feelings again, let alone four times over. Four times more regret to deal with than he already had. There wasn't a day went by that he didn't think about the Korengal job.

'So far, we have nothing to indicate they'll be moved,' Powell said. 'Would you agree?'

Allen nodded. 'Aye. Sounds right.'

'But we've tapped the line they used to make the ransom, and we can access the phone's microphone when it's turned on. So far, that's not happened. As we get more information, you'll get it.'

'We need to go in, like now.' Banks was right. 'We need to get eyes on to confirm if the hostages are there or not.'

Coates stepped forward. 'For now, we don't. Tonight we're going to move to a forward operating base in Fayzabad, which is, flight time, 30 minutes to the target area. We'll wait there for the go or no-go.'

No one said anything.

'I'm going to be honest with you, gents,' Coates went on. 'The use of SF for hostage rescue is not exactly the flavour of the month.'

He had the sense of diplomacy not to mention the failed Korengal job, but everyone in the room knew what he was referring to. 'There are a lot of people in both our governments who think that raids are too messy for public consumption, and that we should start paying ransoms – and that's not good on so many levels. We need to show the world that fucking with our people has consequences. But we have to wait for higher powers to agree that with us.'

There was a ripple of agreement through the room. Allen was one of the men nodding.

Nothing said 'consequence' like a bullet to the face.

CHAPTER 25

Allen packed the last of his items into his bergen, pulled it onto his shoulders and picked up his weapon. 'I'm going to wait on the pad.'

'We don't fly for another hour.'

'I'm going to wait there, all right?'

Taff knew better than to argue with Allen when he was in this kind of mood. Even among the special forces, all of whom were dedicated to their jobs, Allen had a reputation of being as single-minded as a laser. But what they didn't know was that his thoughts weren't about this job, they were about the last one.

'All right,' Taff said. 'I'll see you up there.'

Allen was the first to the pad. There was no sign of the Chinooks that had brought them. Instead, American Black Hawk helicopters were being looked over by the aircrews. Allen watched them doing their pre-flight inspections. Allen had a lot of respect for American airmen, particularly the ones who risked their lives to fly into hot situations to rescue wounded soldiers in contact. He knew that a lot of Americans had risked – even given – their lives to save those of their British allies. Allen had no problem with Americans. He had really enjoyed his time with the SEALs and had even played with the idea of moving to the US to start a new life once his time was served.

He saw someone walking across the pad and recognised the outline of the man immediately.

'Al.' The squadron sergeant major waited until he got closer. 'Stand down. You're not flying tonight. You're staying here. Back to the briefing room, mate.'

Baz's style might have been casual and matey, but familiarity was the way in SF. However, it didn't breed contempt; everyone understood the system that looked to outsiders as slack. What they didn't understand, and what SF did, was that the SSM was still giving an order. Both men had to be respected and obeyed for the system to work.

'You know why?'

'Nah.'

Allen dumped his weapon and kit in the accommodation and headed to the briefing room. As he pushed through the door he saw a lone body sitting and nursing a coffee.

Alex Banks turned in his plastic fold-down chair to see who was joining him, but neither man had time to ask the other what the fuck was going on.

Vasquez appeared just two steps behind Allen. 'Hey, Banks and Allen, right?'

The two men nodded.

Vasquez kept the door open for the two men. 'It's just a short walk.'

As they exited the building, the Black Hawks, with their teams on board, took off as one for forward operating base (FOB) Fayzabad.

CHAPTER 26

Founded in 1981, the 160th Special Operations Aviation Regiment (SOAR) provided helicopter support to US Special Operations missions, and in the Global War on Terror that meant a lot of flying. The 160th operated all over the world, but Afghanistan and Iraq had become their bread and butter. The unit, based out of Fort Campbell, Kentucky, had earned themselves the nickname 'The Night Stalkers' because of their low, fast flying at night, dropping JSOC units onto unsuspecting enemy targets. The aircrews were highly skilled and motivated, and had pulled off incredible feats of piloting. Buffeted by winds, 160th crews had held their aircraft beside cliffs and placed their tail ramps onto the top of mountain peaks. In Iraq, they fitted their aircraft into spaces that most people would struggle to park their car in. The pilots and their crews were an elite, having gone through exceptionally difficult screening and training. But they had to be, by the very nature of the troop tasks that they operated with.

It was the 160th who had carried SEAL Team Six into Pakistan so that they could kill the world's most wanted man, Osama bin Laden. When the Western world wanted a bad guy captured or killed, it was usually the 160th who took the troops into battle. And when there was a hostage being held by armed men, it was the 160th who carried the rescue party.

There had been a cost to this involvement. Nightstalker crews had given their lives on missions and in training.

The SOAR flew a variety of aircraft. The MD 500 Defenders, often known as Little Birds, had been invaluable in Iraq. Special forces operators had sat on benches on either side of the aircraft, with their feet on its skids. The Little Birds had zipped around cities like Baghdad, allowing fighters like Delta Force to be placed directly onto rooftops or in the narrow streets that made up the city's labyrinth. The Night Stalkers also flew the big, twin-rotored CH-47 Chinooks, which allowed for a large number of men and equipment to be transported. In between these aircraft in size and mobility was the UH-60 Black Hawk, a medium lift utility helicopter that had served the United States and other militaries all over the world.

Two Apache gunships rode shotgun to the four Black Hawks. By the time Allen and Banks had walked out of the briefing room to wherever Vasquez was taking them. The gunships were already in the air, providing cover for the Black Hawks' lift.

CHAPTER 27

Lieutenant Steve Ream didn't have an ounce of quit in him. Born and raised in Atlanta, Georgia, Ream had joined the service in 2005, and first saw active duty in Iraq as an army helicopter pilot. He had then volunteered for selection to the 160th, which filtered out the great pilots from the very good. This was his second rotation in Afghanistan, where he had spent much of his time flying special operations forces in and out of direct action missions. Ream had seen a few things. Heavy gunfights. Air strikes. Blood washed out of the back of his aircraft after the wounded and dead had been pulled on board. Ream always shared that duty with his door gunners. It was a hard thing to wash away the blood of your countrymen, but that was precisely why he did it. A good leader should never ask his men to do anything that he wasn't willing to do himself.

Ream didn't expect any trouble tonight – this was about as routine as it got in the 160th, flying a task force from one base to another – but in a day or maybe a week it could be a very different story. If the hostage rescue mission got the go, that would require fast and low flying through some of the most rugged terrain on earth. The thought of it excited him. No one was in special operations for easy. The real world didn't understand people like Ream. It wasn't some gung-ho comic strip bullshit that made him feel the way he did. The instinct to fight had helped us become successful as a species. In men like Ream, their instinct wasn't highly- or even under-developed, it just hadn't been diluted.

The pilot looked through the canopy of his cockpit and at the skies above Afghanistan. It was already a brilliant sky, untouched by light pollution, but the night-vision goggles he wore picked up even more stars than the human eye could. Millions of pinpricks of light were all around him. It was an incredible sight. One that brought the religious man closer to God. Ream had been brought up in a churchgoing family and war had only cemented his faith. As the old saying went, there are no atheists in foxholes. Ream had seen enough to know that there were no atheists in a helicopter taking fire, either. The thought of crashing to the ground turned a man into a believer really quickly.

Ream leaned around and looked into the back of his aircraft. The rear of the Black Hawk was packed full of bearded British soldiers. Some were asleep. Some were looking out at the sky, maybe deep in thought, maybe enjoying the same stars as he was. He always enjoyed talking with Brits, even if he didn't understand what they were saying: some of their accents were so difficult to understand Ream wasn't even sure if they were speaking English. What he was sure of was their professionalism. They and the Aussies were as good as any unit he'd ever worked with.

The pilot looked back at his navigation screen. They were about to cross from Takhar Province into Badakhshan. Soon Ream would begin to drop height to set down in the small FOB on the outskirts of Fayzabad. He'd been told that the Taliban weren't highly active in the area, and not to expect fire, but Ream's number-one rule for staying alive was always to expect the worst, and pray for the best. It had served him well in life so far. He had a loving wife, two healthy kids and a job where he could serve his country. Ream was proud of his service, but this could be his first hostage rescue. God willing, the 160th crews would bring them all back safely.

When Ream saw the forests and the jagged mountains ahead of them, he wondered just how likely that would be.

Badakhshan was a defender's dream.

CHAPTER 28

In the back of one of the Black Hawks, Miller sat with his thoughts, and they were troubled.

The Korengal job was preying on his mind, but not like it did with Allen. Miller's thoughts were about risk and reward. He still couldn't reconcile risking himself and his friends for so few who had no tactical importance, and who had put themselves in danger. Miller didn't think that way, but then he wasn't a politician. He was in-country to fight and not be killed while sorting out the self-made problems of others, and that should happen in the fight. It wasn't the death in the Korengal that was a problem for Miller. It was that he might be taking risks with no reward once again.

When Miller had signed up for the military on 9/12, he'd done so with the expectation that he was signing his own death warrant, and he was okay with that. Some things were worth dying for. Family. Friends. Freedom. His country. There was an old cowboy who'd been in special operations during Vietnam, crossing the border into Laos on Black Ops. He'd told Miller stories about combat and his thoughts on what made a warrior. In that man's mind, a man can't truly become a warrior until he accepts the fact that he isn't going to make it home. Only then can he do 'warrior things'.

The 32-year-old SEAL had done a lot of warrior things since he'd joined the teams, and he had the medals to show for it. Miller had never sought higher rank, happy to do his part as an assaulter. Truth be told, he thought the war would have been over by now, but more enemies kept popping up, and so he would do his part in knocking them back down. He was the property of the US Navy, body and soul, until they told him otherwise. He was fighting because his country needed him to. He missed the mountains of home, the herds of cattle, country music bars and cowgirls. As soon as there was peace, he would be a peaceful man.

Until that day came, Miller would be a warrior.

CHAPTER 29

BAGRAM

Vasquez offered Banks and Allen seats on the other side of his desk.

'Smoke?'

Both men gave a wave off and a 'No thanks.'

Vasquez lit up and passed the Newports to Powell, who joined him. She had decided that she was just bluffing herself that she was really trying to give up.

'This room's as secure as any in Kabul,' Vasquez told them. 'Swept for listening devices, thick walls, no windows, no comms equipment that can get tapped into.'

Vasquez smiled as he glanced at Powell before addressing the two men.

'So, we were thinking about the two guys with the most questions and thought that maybe they can go and find the answers.'

He had thought about that one-liner but it didn't get the reaction he was hoping for from the two men sitting in front of him. Powell still thought it was a good one.

'Sergeant Allen,' Powell went on in a formal way that she thought would be correct. They didn't know each other and she wanted to show respect. 'As you said yourself, there's no way for us to know the layout of the cave, or how many men exactly are inside. We still have drone coverage, but they can't see through rock.'

'You want us to recce the area?' Allen asked hopefully.

When Powell nodded, Allen was mentally grinning like the Cheshire Cat.

'This is a hostage rescue mission,' Vasquez finished for her. 'And our governments don't want another hostage bad news story to spin.'

'If we get the go, all that matters is getting the hostages out safe and sound,' Vasquez continued. 'I'd be super happy if you also kill the fuckers. We don't see any of that happening unless we have some idea of where they're located in the caves. We need information, gents. Information to plan and execute the rescue. If we get the go, of course.'

'Why us?' Banks asked. 'There are better recon men in the unit than me.'

'But are there better parachutists?' Vasquez asked back. 'We were told that you were the most experienced in your unit. Where you'll be jumping into are valleys full of unpredictable crosswinds, and the best landing site you're going to find needs also to be able to take the Black Hawks.'

'We can't go in by helicopter, land way out and move on foot to target?' Banks asked, and Vasquez shook his head.

'Any helicopter activity beyond the FOB at Fayzabad would be flagged up and might scare the kidnappers. Then who knows what they would do? And remember, Captain Coates said it's not just the hostages' lives at stake here. It's the future of special operations involvement in hostage rescue.'

'Understood,' Banks said.

'So, you guys up for some night jumping?'

Allen raised a smile. 'Sounds like a great night out.' He turned to Banks. 'Doesn't it, mate?'

Powell stubbed her cigarette butt in the shell casing with a smile even bigger than Allen's, and Vasquez laughed to himself as he stood from his chair. 'The riggers, they're standing by.'

CHAPTER 30

BADAKHSHAN

Umid sat around the fire with the other bandits. For the first time since they had set off on their mission, the mood was sour. It had been more than a day since they had given their ransom demand to the Afghan government, but there had been no word from Jallah that he had been released and not one dollar had been delivered.

'They're stalling,' Daler said. 'They are playing for time.'

'They're the government,' someone else said. 'They don't do anything quickly.'

Umid looked at Sherali. Their leader was saying nothing. Sherali was watching the flames of the fire and stroking his beard.

'Maybe it takes time for them to get the money?' Umid said. 'It's a lot.'

'It's a lot for you and me,' Daler replied, 'but not for them. Money is like water to these people. They bathe in it. I'm telling you, they're stalling. The longer they drag things out, the longer they have to find us.'

'Why would they want to find us?' Umid asked innocently.

'Why do you think?' Daler laughed. 'To send their special forces. They come in black helicopters and with black faces. They take people from their homes, and they are never seen again.'

'Like Jallah?'

Daler nodded. 'Like Jallah. For a time the Americans went after the opium crops, burning them and imprisoning the smugglers.'

'Why did they stop?'

One of the bandits laughed. 'Because without crops to farm, a man must pick up a rifle. I would know,' he said. 'I am one of them.'

'A man needs money,' Daler said, 'and right now we have none. We are placing ourselves at great risk here, friends, and willingly, but we do so for reward. Sherali, is it not time that we made an example?'

Sherali continued to look into the fire. 'And what kind of example were you thinking, Daler?'

'Kill one of the hostages.'

'They're worth nothing dead.'

'They don't care about the Afghans,' Daler said. 'So long as we don't harm the white and the black woman they will pay a ransom.'

'If they don't care about the Afghans, then why would they be moved to act any faster?'

For a moment Daler didn't reply. 'The white woman,' he said at last. 'We could cut off her nose and ears.'

No one said anything. The sick feeling in Umid's stomach protested, but not his mouth.

'These things take time,' Sherali said, ending the subject. 'And as time goes by, we will consider all possibilities.'

Daler nodded to his leader in deference, accepting his decision. A moment later, Sherali turned on his phone and made a call.

It was to their contact in Fayzabad. Sherali listened, looked grave, hung up, then spoke.

'Brothers,' he said calmly, 'six American helicopters have flown into the base at Fayzabad. Two of them are mosquitoes. I don't need to tell you that this is very unusual for that camp.'

'What does it mean?' Umid asked him.

Sherali's answer was simple. 'It means that we're being hunted.'

CHAPTER 31

BAGRAM

In the stores, the two men met up with the riggers who were responsible for packing their parachutes and preparing the kit needed for a high-altitude jump.

As Air Troop's sergeant, Allen had a thousand-plus jumps under his belt. Some men hated jumping, conquering fear to jump anyway, but Allen had found he had a passion for jumping out of perfectly good aircraft. It wasn't quite the intensity of combat, but it wasn't far behind. Particularly a jump like this, into a dangerous environment and a restricted LS, and at night. Allen was under no false impressions: mess this up and he would be dead by morning.

He went over the kit again and again. Each item would be critical for his survival. The function of the main canopy and reserve spoke for itself: without the skills of the riggers who had packed them, Allen would be a red stain on an Afghan hillside. Allen checked the hooks and straps of the parachute harness, and just as crucial, the three-ring circus, the two steel devices that connected the canopy's lines. Allen re-checked them all. It was no good if the canopy opened and Allen fell out of his harness, or lines just fell away. That landing would be his last.

The two altimeters, always doubling up in case of malfunction, worn on the outside of the clothing on

Allen's wrists, were vital for high altitude, high opening (HAHO) jumps.

Allen and Banks would be jumping from 35,000 feet, which was about the height that a commercial airliner cruised at. In this part of the world, which included the Hindu Kush and tall mountain ranges, military free fall was pushed to its upper limits. So high in the atmosphere, Allen and Banks would require oxygen in free fall. If there was any issue with that equipment they would black out from hypoxia: lack of oxygen in the blood. Best case scenario, they'd wake up in the lower atmosphere, way off target, and recover their wits quickly enough to land somewhere safely, and try to make it on foot to target. Worst case … they'd never wake up.

There were a lot of bad things that could happen on a HAHO jump. The goggles were to stop Allen's eyeballs from freezing in their sockets, and the cold and wind proofs were to stop him from getting frostbite on his extremities or suffering from hypothermia. The temperature at 35,000 feet was around –44°C, and though it would warm as the men dropped altitude, they would still be exposed to freezing conditions as they cruised the 30,000 feet under canopy to the target.

Allen and Banks had agreed on HAHO over HALO (high altitude, low opening) for one simple reason: it would allow the aircraft that dropped them to fly at a greater distance from the target and so lessen any compromise. They'd open high and glide in.

As well as their parachuting equipment, they were jumping with everything they needed to set up an observation post (OP), and fight, if needed. Allen thought back to the American SEALs who had been discovered in the nearby Kunar Province, where only one had lived to tell the tale. It was a story that the SEALs could be rightly proud of: not only had the team fought valiantly, but its commander had given his own life to call in support. For his actions, he was given America's highest award, the Medal of Honor.

Allen had a few medals of his own but he didn't want to add a posthumous one, not if he could help it. He filled nine magazines for his carbine, and packed another 300 rounds in bandoliers. As well as three magazines for his 9mm sidearm, he checked and packed three smoke grenades, each a different colour as markers for aircraft, and two fragmentation grenades: one for the enemy and one for himself if he was captured. Allen accepted the possibility of death as a part of the job, but he wouldn't let himself fall into enemy hands to be beheaded on camera. If all hope was lost, he'd hold the final grenade to his chest and try and take a couple more with him.

On top of this heavy load of ammunition came water and rations for five days, which could be made to stretch for longer if need be. As a kid with an alcoholic father and a mother who worked all hours to support the family, Allen knew hunger, and that it could be beaten with strength of mind, at least for a while. He also took camouflage netting, collapsible poles, hessian, and a small pick and a shovel for creating the OP.

Finally, for his weapon, Allen chose an ACOG (Advanced Combat Optical Gun) sight for day, and a thermal sight for night. A laser light module, torch and foregrip were added to his rifle. The final piece of kit was a fighting knife that Allen sheathed on his plate carrier. If there was silent killing to be done, then it would be done with a blade. The SAS had a winged dagger as its insignia for a reason.

By the time the kit was packed, most men would have struggled to lift it, but Allen and Banks were not most men. Both of their nations had long histories of producing warriors and winning wars. As Allen had once been told by an instructor, 'Selection is the easy part. Wait until you try war.'

Of course, there had been nothing easy about special forces selection. It tested men to their limits, and very few had what it took to pass, but that was the point: selection was the minimum standard. Every man in a Tier 1 unit had passed it. If you wanted to stand out in a unit like the SAS, you needed to find another level again, and again, and again. You were only as good as your last job, and your position in the regiment was never truly safe.

Allen checked the quick-release handles on his hooks, the two devices that connected his bergen below the parachute pack. Finally happy, he looked across the stores at Banks.

'You ready?' he asked him.

The SEAL shouldered his heavy kit with ease and walked towards the door and the glaring sunshine beyond.

Allen watched him go and smiled. He had always loved competition.

CHAPTER 32

FOB FAYZABAD, BADAKHSHAN

As Allen and Banks were preparing their equipment in Bagram, the other SEALs and SAS troopers were settling into the FOB.

The forward operating base reflected the nature of the conflict in the province. Unlike provinces such as Helmand, there were no battalions of infantry onsite. The small base was used for intelligence gathering, and as a footprint to enable interaction with the local populace. It was not, ordinarily, a launch point for fighting troops, but the four Black Hawks and two Apaches on the helicopter landing zone said loud and clear that this was soon to change.

As with all operations, the men were taking the chance to eat and sleep when they could: in war, you never know when your next hot meal is coming or when you will next get your head down.

The teams and all the aircrews were on five minutes' notice to move if the Emergency Response was called by the ops room. The ER was a smash-and-grab of the hostages, acting with just the information of the target they knew at the time. It was a simple drill because it had to be. Just like it would be in a fire station, all the team's kit was packed, laid out and ready to go. All weapons were made ready and all radio batteries were fully charged. The teams and aircrews would sleep in their clothing and boots so that when rotors started turning the troops would be inside the Black Hawks within five minutes. A few minutes later, the aircraft with their Apache cover would have their rotors at full speed and be taking off. All briefing would be given over the net as they headed for the target. Being stood to for an ER was part of SF life. Sometimes for days, even weeks, at a time. But once forward on the ground, they had to be always ready: situations change higher up the food chain and no one wants to be caught with their pants down if they are ordered to assault.

In the large tent that served as the FOB's cookhouse, Miller took his tray of food and looked for a table to sit at. In many ways military cookhouses were the same as school canteens. There were groups of friends, and cliques. Seniors mostly mixed with men their own rank, and the same with juniors. Sometimes a man would be sitting alone.

As a ranch hand back in Montana, Miller had found himself eating alone as he bounced between ranches looking for seasonal work. The ranch crews were as close knit as a SEAL team, and a man had to earn his place. Until then, a person ate alone, and Miller didn't like eating alone. It felt wrong. Unnatural, even. 'Breaking bread' with another person was an important part of culture stretching back through history, and Miller reckoned there was a lot to be learned from studying history, and people.

'You mind?' he asked Taff, who was the only person sitting at the long fold-down trestle table. The three mates the Welshman had been eating with had already left. He was on his own, but not lonely. He just wanted to have a quiet coffee, but that wasn't to be.

'Course not.' The SAS trooper pointed at the man standing with his hands balancing his steel portion tray of meat loaf and mash. 'Miller, yeah?'

'Yessir,' the American replied as he took a seat on the bench opposite Taff.

'I'm not an officer, mate, you don't need to call me sir.'

Miller smiled. 'I know that, but where I'm from, sir isn't just for officers. A guy pumping gas, your mailman, the man serving you a beer, those are all sirs if you respect them, and my pa told me you always respect a man until he gives you a reason not to.'

'Sounds like a sound man, your dad.'

'No sir, not at all. Yours?'

'Used to beat the shit out of me like I was the regimental band's drum.' Taff smiled. He'd learned a long time ago to hide the pain of his childhood behind jokes, smiles and achievements.

'I hear you, brother.'

Sometimes Taff even wondered if he could have made it to the SAS without his father's treatment. The old man had certainly introduced him to pain at an early age, and forced him to become mentally tough. Taff knew there were people from all kinds of backgrounds in the special forces – good homes and bad – and he was astute enough to recognise that he had cottoned on to Allen as a mentor because the Scotsman possessed many of the characteristics that his father had lacked: integrity, control, calmness.

Miller and Taff then ate and drank in silence. What more was there to say?

Both men finished, then Miller pushed his tray into the middle of the table to place a tin of dip on it before offering Taff first pinch.

'You're all right, mate, not for me.'

The two men had bonded tight.

CHAPTER 33

In the skies above Miller and Taff, a giant Lockheed Martin C-130J Hercules was making its way to the northeast of Afghanistan. The four-engine turboprop aircraft had been a mainstay of militaries since its introduction to service in 1956. The airframe had been updated and refitted, but the role of the 'Hercules' remained the same: as a versatile transport aircraft capable of delivering anything from humanitarian aid on unprepared runways to dropping paratroopers after a low-level insertion. The latest C-130J version could carry and deploy 64 airborne troops, but this evening, as the sun set across the mountains of the country, only two men were preparing to jump.

They got slowly to their feet and gripped the airframe to steady themselves. It wasn't easy. Each of them was carrying 65 kilos of equipment, including their oxygen supply. They stood as still as they could while the loadmasters carried out their final checks on the two jumpers' rigs.

Allen did what he normally did at this point and checked that his made-ready HK carbine was still nice and tight against his body. The state of a weapon was important to all soldiers to prevent them from accidentally shooting each other. Safe: no magazine on the weapon and no round in the chamber. Loaded: a magazine loaded with rounds is on the weapon but no round in the chamber. Made Ready: a loaded magazine on the weapon and a round in the chamber.

It was strapped over his left shoulder with the barrel facing down. The rig was then put on over it to make sure the weapon wasn't going anywhere. It wasn't, but he always checked anyway. Most jumpers had a ritual. Once that was done he stared down at his boots as the loadmasters' weak red torchlights flitted about his rig.

First was the pin checks. These two shafts of steel were connected by steel wires to the two red handles that needed to be pulled to deploy the main canopy and reserve. They needed to be seated properly in the loop of paracord that kept both canopies inside the rig. Sometimes they could get stuck; a handle was pulled, it wasn't going anywhere. Or it was almost out of the paracord loop and so the canopy could pop while on the ramp, dragging the jumper out prematurely, or popping the canopy too early during the free fall. Not a great day out on either account.

The next bit of kit to be checked was the automatic opening device (AOD).

This mechanical box worked by measuring the barometric pressure and was set to pull the main canopy's pin at 3,000 feet if the jumper wasn't able to function and pull his own canopy. It could be unconsciousness due to a mid-air collision, or the jumper simply couldn't get his hand to the handle to pull. It had happened, and in these cases the AOD would do it for them. Another possible cause for the jumper being incapacitated was hypoxia.

When Allen had first learned to jump, his team were sent to RAF North Luffenham, the RAF medical centre, for chest X-rays and lectures about the signs and symptoms of hypoxia – and warnings about what would happen if their teeth were not in good condition. A small air pocket in a filling would expand with altitude, until finally the tooth exploded. Allen had seen it happen twice to other people and it was nasty.

They then spent time in a decompression chamber, doing exactly the opposite of what divers do, gradually being starved of oxygen. They sat there chatting away and were asked to do their 10 times table and draw pictures of pigs and elephants. Allen's elephants were outrageous, with disproportionately big eyes. Then, as the chamber drained of oxygen, his 10 times table went completely to rat shit; he felt himself getting slow and lethargic. The moment he was allowed to put his mask back on and take a breath, it all came good again. Apart from the elephant; the monster with big eyes was the best he could do under any conditions.

Members of Air Troop would have to go to RAF North Luffenham once a year for the rest of their careers in order to keep their free-fall qualification. Every year they would have to go through the same lecture, have another set of chest X-rays and have their ears checked; if they couldn't clear the pressure in their ears they'd be heading for major dramas.

The loadies' last check was to ensure that the hooks were secure. These attached Allen's bergen to his rig and dangled below it and behind his legs.

He got a hard slap on the shoulder. All was good on his rig. The red torchlight moved in front of him, and the loadie placed a gloved finger on his oxygen bottle indicator. It was Allen's cue to look at it himself and acknowledge with a firm nod.

Yes, the bottle was open, and yes, he was breathing oxygen, and yes, the bottle was full.

There was nothing either of them could do for the next few minutes but keep a tight grip on the airframe to make life just a little more comfortable, and to look down, stare at their boots and zone out. Life would be busy soon enough.

It was maybe just over three minutes when the loadies made a sweep with their torchlights to make sure there was nothing loose that could be sucked out as soon as the ramp opened.

Another minute passed, and then Allen and Banks were once more slapped on the shoulder, and this time indicated towards the still-closed ramp. It was pointless shouting commands; the aircraft noise was deafening and the jumpers' helmets made everything sound muffled.

The two men waddled towards the rear of the aircraft like a pair of geese, placing weight deliberately on each foot in turn, the kit on their upper bodies pushing down on them, and their bergens against the backs of their legs inhibiting movement.

When both men were almost at the ramp, a loadie off to their left and a little ahead of them spoke into his headset and the ramp began to move. Even through his helmet Allen heard the massive rush and a split second later a gale was thrashing against him as the four Rolls-Royce turboprops thrust the aircraft through the air.

Allen glanced across to Banks. The SEAL made for an impressive figure. Hidden behind the goggles and mask, and weighed down in kit, he looked like something from a science fiction movie. No doubt about it, what they were about to do was on the cutting edge of military technology, but when it came down to it, none of the tactics and equipment mattered unless you had the guts to jump. Warfare could change, but not the warrior. Without courage, nothing else mattered.

Above 30,000 feet, the northern provinces were spread out beneath them as a series of bumpy peaks surrounded by flattened valleys, the entire landscape touched orange by the setting sun. From up high it all looked beautiful, but Allen knew that soon those mountains would be trying to kill him. Jumping into landscapes like this was dangerous at the best of times, and by the time that Allen and Banks landed night would have fallen. They'd timed their insertion so that they could get as much help with the light as possible, but by the time that they hit 5,000 feet they needed darkness to help protect them from prying eyes.

Allen adjusted the oxygen mask on his face. His neck and ears were covered by a 5mm thick neoprene balaclava that sat beneath his helmet, but he could feel the cold biting at the millimetres of exposed skin between mask and goggles. The weight of his gear on him pulled him down like an anchor.

Allen thought back to the planning session at Bagram. He and Banks had gone over satellite photos, maps and meteorological reports to choose their landing zone. The SEAL knew his business well, quickly deducing where they would need to jump to account for changing air currents as they descended. Basic military parachuting static line didn't involve much more than the courage you needed to throw yourself out of the aircraft, and the luck required to land on something soft. HAHO was a different beast. Of course, the need for courage remained, but there was no way that you could jump from more than 30,000 feet and hope to hit your landing site (LS).

The jump needed to be planned with mathematical precision. How long until they deployed their canopies? How far would the wind carry them in one direction? How high did they need to be to clear any peaks and ridges on 'finals'? This was the route they would try and take over the LS so they landed into the wind and so made a safe landing. The LS that the two jumpers had identified was at the end of a narrow pass between steep, unforgiving mountains. Better sites existed, but they were too close to sites of habitation, or too far from the target, and had to be able to take the Black Hawks. Their chosen LS was the only chance of getting eyes on the target that night. It also meant that, for the teams, there would be a proven route to target. It also meant that they would risk broken bones, and worse, but that was the job. If it was easy then anyone could do it, and Allen and Banks wouldn't be needed on the 130's ramp in the first place.

Secured to the frame of the aircraft by a webbing strap, the loadmaster positioned himself slightly in front of the two jumpers and held out an arm – not as a barrier from the emptiness beyond, but as an indicator to stop where they were. If the aircraft jerked because the pilots had to quickly adjust their path, there was always a possibility that jumpers with such heavy kit, unable to support themselves correctly, could topple off the ramp. Even the strongest loadie's arm wasn't going to stop that from happening.

Allen peered down once more, and the landscape beyond

the ramp was now shrouded in gloom. The sun had set, and night was falling. He just wanted to get out and into the air; he, and no doubt Banks, hated standing on the ramp in full kit. It was a pain in the arse trying to keep stable as the aircraft jostled about to get on the correct bearing for the jump. Now the only thing the men needed to do was focus on the jump lights. The ramp had two sets, one on each side. They were nice and high so they could be seen even by jumpers at the back of a large stack.

The loadie jerked a finger up as the first light illuminated. 'Red on! Red on!'

Allen couldn't hear him but that didn't matter. Both men joined in with a loud scream through their oxygen masks: 'Red on! Red on!'

Allen had never known why this was the protocol, since no one could hear anything; it was just something that always happened.

The aircraft jinked sideways, and Allen and Banks gripped each other's arm to stabilise themselves as they waddled the last couple of steps to the very edge of the ramp.

Two sets of eyes were glued on the red lights waiting for them to change.

Less than 30 seconds later they did.

'*Green on!*' The loadie was shouting it out and pointing, but that didn't matter. The two men were now in control of themselves. The moment the light had changed, the men's eyes drilled into each other as they screamed in unison: '*Ready!*'

They rocked forward, screaming above the roar: '*Set!*'

They rocked back. '*Go!*'

Both men dribbled off the ramp. There was never any finesse exiting the ramp in full kit.

Allen felt the slipstream pick him up and toss him about but it wasn't long before he was clear of it and could sort himself out. He could tell by the wind force pushing his arms and legs up rather than out that he was upside down. But that wasn't a problem; Allen never worried too much if he became unstable on exit. Getting off the ramp cleanly was the most important thing for him. He simply spread out his arms and legs and as soon as he arched his back, he had banged himself over into a stable face-down position.

He looked around – moving your head during free fall is about the only thing that doesn't have an effect on stability – trying to see where Banks was before he lost him in the darkness. To his right and above he spotted him, also unstable and banging himself over. Allen looked above Banks. He could no longer see the C-130, not that he expected to. There would be no navigation lights. He looked below, where the peaks and valleys of Badakhshan were blanketed in darkness and where there were also no lights to be seen.

CHAPTER 34

It was Umid's turn to stand watch over the guests. He preferred to think of them that way, and not as hostages or prisoners. After all, the women had not been beaten, or worse. They were being fed and sheltered. They wanted to be let go, he knew that, but in his homeland it was not the place of a woman to get what she wanted, but to do what a man told her to do. And so, in truth, he saw very little difference in their situation, and the situation of most women in his country. That was just the way of things, and it was not his place to question it. Umid loved his mother, but it was to his father that he deferred. When his father left this life, then Umid would defer to his oldest brother. That his mother was older did not mean that she was wiser. There were some things that only a man could be trusted with. Umid had been told this all his life.

He wondered how things would be different if it were four men that they had taken to the cave. Would his compatriots have been kinder to them or more violent? Would the guests have struggled? Would they have forced the hand of Umid and the others, and died trying to escape? Umid thought of his father and older brothers. He couldn't picture them sitting here meekly. But then again, Jallah was in such a position, held by the Americans. It was his release that this enterprise had been designed to ensure. Jallah hadn't died fighting. Maybe he was behaving just as these women were.

Umid had asked his leader, Sherali, about Jallah. 'He is a close friend of our patron,' the old bandit had told him. 'They are like brothers, their families tied through marriages, and through business. Our patron is honour-bound to do every-thing he can to get Jallah back.'

'He would do the same for you?' Umid had asked, expect-ing a simple yes. Instead, Sherali had smiled.

'There are bandit lords, and then there are simply bandits. I am a simple man, Umid, and so I will have a simple fate.'

Umid nodded, unwilling to disagree with Sherali, even if it was to tell him that he was far from a simple man. After all, Sherali was a mujahid. He was a special man, even if he would not admit so himself. His humbleness made Umid like him all the more.

'Excuse me,' someone said. It was Tasneem, the oldest of the women.

'Yes?'

'May we have some more water?' She held up the empty bowl. Umid didn't like that the guests were having to drink from it, but there were only a few tin cups to be shared between them all.

'I'll bring some when I am relieved,' Umid told her. In his culture, modesty, loyalty and hospitality were marks by which a man was judged. Umid remembered when, as a young boy, his family had gone hungry for days following the arrival of guests, to whom his father would not deny shelter and food, even if it came at the expense of his own household. 'Anyone can be generous when they can afford it,' he had told his sons. 'What matters is how generous you are when you have nothing to give.'

Umid had been thinking a lot about his father since they had come to the cave. What would he think about their situation? He had no doubt that his father would approve of the modest and brave Sherali, but he couldn't help feeling a pang of doubt. To his knowledge, his father had never taken people against their will in order to ransom them. Of course, no son knows all of his father's stories, but Umid could not reconcile the action with what he knew of his father. Somehow it felt … beneath him.

Lost in his own thoughts, Umid suddenly realised that Tasneem's eyes were still on him.

'I promise I will bring you water when I am relieved,' he told her.

She shook her head gently. 'It's not that,' she said. 'I was thinking about how you remind me of my own son.'

'You have sons?'

'Of course. I have four children. The oldest is your age. The youngest is 12.'

Umid frowned. 'Then why would you leave them?'

'This is what I ask myself every day. The truth is that, many days, I wish that I had not. But then I remind myself that my children have been my greatest joy. My reason for living. With that being so, if I can help others to know that joy, then I have a duty to set aside my own happiness in the short term for the long-term happiness of a stranger. Every young child that dies could have grown into someone like my son … or you.'

Umid said nothing.

'You treat us like guests.' Tasneem smiled her thanks, making her insight even more frightening to Umid. 'You live by a code, to treat people with respect and hospitality, no matter the circumstances. Well, that is how I see my own code, too. Except that I travel to find those situations.'

It made a lot of sense to Umid. So much so that he didn't know what to say.

'Oh, I'm not asking you for any favours, Umid. Don't fear. I would never think to test your loyalty. I am just speaking out loud because it makes me feel better, that's all. It makes me feel like a person, and not a tethered dog.'

'You're not tethered.'

'No ...' Tasneem said sadly, 'but I would not be allowed to walk from here, would I?'

Umid understood then. She was tethered after all.

'What is she like?' he asked, changing the subject. 'The English woman?'

Tasneem looked to where the other hostages were huddled and sleeping on dusty blankets.

'She is a good woman. Different, but the same. She wants the same as I do.'

'Do they have no problems in her own country?' Umid asked. 'No sickness?'

'They have both.'

'Then I don't understand. Why does she come here, instead of helping her own people?'

'Because she sees us as her own people too,' Tasneem explained. 'She does not believe in borders, or tribes, or clans. She believes that we are all one family.'

Umid shook his head at the stupidity of it. Many of the men in his group believed that a white person in their land could only mean one thing: a spy for the Americans. Umid had far less sympathy for her than he had for Tasneem. The Afghan woman he felt was misguided. She should have stayed in her home, but obviously she lacked strong men in her family to keep her there. The white woman had no business in Afghanistan, and he told Tasneem as much.

'But she is here. And she is your guest.'

'She is,' Umid agreed. 'For now.'

CHAPTER 35

Allen was as close to being an astronaut as he ever would be. He'd jumped at 32,000 feet into the tropopause, the earth's second layer of atmosphere. Most people who were at this height were on passenger planes, not free falling through the sky at terminal velocity. All he could hear was the rush of air; it was like sticking his head out of a car travelling at 120mph. All he had to do now was keep stable on heading, not moving about the sky or turning, no matter how slow, and wait until he reached his pulling altitude.

Barometric pressure was noticeably less at this altitude, making Allen feel lighter, and colder. Even through his specialised clothing he could feel the cold air whipping at him, but he wasn't worried about that. He was falling through the physiological deficient zone, where human life cannot survive without adaptations. For this, Allen's oxygen mask and bottle were his lifeline.

Hypoxia starts to affect a body as the amount of oxygen in the blood decreases much more rapidly at 10,000 feet above sea level, and a human's night vision sensitivity decreases by 30 per cent. At 20,000 feet the jumper is in critical condition. If Allen's oxygen supply failed, he would have as little as a few minutes before he lost muscle coordination and consciousness. If he hadn't already deployed his canopy by

3,600 feet, his AOD would pull the pin out and the canopy would deploy. He would then be taken by the winds and drift far off target, possibly even into a neighbouring country, many of which lay close to Badakhshan Province. If he was unconscious for landing, Allen could expect severe injury and broken bones, and that would be at best; he would likely not survive. There was no safe moment during HAHO, but some moments were more dangerous than others. Once Allen was out of the critical stage, and no longer relying on his oxygen mask, he could breathe a little easier.

Until he was below 10,000 feet, lack of oxygen was Allen's greatest enemy.

Things started well. The exit from the aircraft was clean. Allen could see Banks falling at the same velocity off his right-hand side. Both men were stable on heading, in controlled falls. So far so good.

Watching his left-hand altimeter, and with a check to make sure that Banks had not closed up to a position where there would be a collision, Allen prepared to 'dump' his canopy.

He moved his left hand up, just above his head, and his right hand down to grip the red steel handle at chest height. There had to be symmetry. If Allen just put one arm out, that would have hit the air and produced the start of a tumble.

Allen was still stable on heading, eyes glued to the needle on his left wrist alti. Bang on 20,000 feet, he pulled the handle and immediately pushed both arms up above his head, which made him backslide almost into a sitting position. The air immediately caught the drogue chute to drag the bag carrying the canopy out quicker. He felt himself rock slightly from side to side as the bag and lines were pulled away from the rig. Then *bang* – the canopy deployed. Allen decelerated from 120mph to hardly anything in just one second. He felt like a cartoon character who'd just run into a wall.

Allen heard Banks's canopy cracking open just above him as he fitted his night-vision goggles (NVGs). Good, he was near.

Now the real work began: navigating their way down to the distant landing site, and all in darkness.

For this Allen used his GPS. It's always the lower man that navigates. This gives the rest of the patrol time to stack up close so they are all under the canopy as a unit and land as one. Banks still had a job to do alongside staying close: he would be check navigating.

The moon had risen and was turning scattered clouds golden in colour. It would be a good night for ambient light, which would raise the effectiveness of the men's NVGs. They needed to have their observation post (OP) in place well before first light, and the moon would help them move faster. But it would also mean that the kidnappers could see better, too. The moonlight would help Allen and Banks in their insertion, but hamper them when it came to setting up their OP. Sometimes the best weather and conditions to operate in were the more harsh, wind and rain keeping people miserable and indoors, but tonight was a beautiful night of late Afghan summer.

As he was considering this, Allen realised that something was wrong. It was a subtle feeling, but he identified the cause quickly: the oxygen wasn't flowing.

Allen's immediate action drill was to check his mask and the hose connection. Nothing had come loose. He turned his attention to the oxygen bottle and checked that the connection was on tight. It was too dark for him to see the level indicator, but the valve was open. The fittings were tight.

Sometimes brute force was the right choice. Allen shook the bottle. Thumped it. Nothing happened.

Allen looked at his altimeter: 17,000 feet. Another 5,000 to go until he could safely breathe without oxygen. Allen had two options: fight off the effects of oxygen deprivation as best as he could, or 'cut away', drop, and dump his reserve.

It took two seconds for him to decide. Dropping his height quickly would see him way off target, and the time line for the OP to be in position would be lost – or worse, the mission would have to be scrubbed. That wasn't going to happen.

Allen did not allow any sense of panic to enter his mind, because then it would enter his body. He needed his breathing slow, and regulated, and fear would make it fast and shallow. Allen simply refused to let emotion rule over him. He closed off his natural instincts, put them in a box and buried them deep inside himself. He was as close to a robot as a man could be. That was how he'd survived in the past. That would be how he survived now.

Allen took long, slow breaths.

Ninety seconds after he detected the fault, Allen began to feel his eyes getting heavy. He wanted to yawn. His oxygen levels were getting lower, but so was he. He just needed to hold out until he lost height.

He fought against the drowsiness, busying his mind with checking his altimeter and GPS. He continued to play with the oxygen tank, mask and line, but to no avail. No matter. He just needed to stay alert.

Allen felt his muscles getting tired. Oxygen wasn't arriving in the tissue as quickly as it would be on the ground. It made his movements slower. He felt like someone had given him a sleeping pill. Every sense was telling him to close his eyes, relax and sleep.

Allen didn't listen.

On hard runs and tabs some soldiers would talk out loud to themselves, as though they were their own drill instructor. Allen had never been one of them. He didn't want to show weakness. He kept his own 'drill instructor' inside himself, a voice in his mind only. He used that voice now.

Stay the fuck awake.

Don't you dare close your eyes.

Don't you fail in front of him. Don't you fucking dare.

The presence of Banks nearby in the sky was a powerful motivator. Allen couldn't live with the shame of being the cause of a scrubbed mission. He knew without doubt that he would rather die than need to be rescued. He would make it to the ground without Banks knowing about this struggle or he would never make it at all. Those were the two options he gave himself, and one option was no option at all.

His only choice was to succeed.

CHAPTER 36

Minutes passed like hours, every one of them a battle of Allen's mind against his body. He pulled away at his mask; it was useless now and he wanted to make sure there wasn't any obstruction between his nose and mouth – and in turn that the little oxygen that was out there was for him.

Allen focused his eyes and mind on the next waypoint on his GPS.

He watched his altimeter. 13,000 feet. 12,000. 11,000.

And then, after a long-fought battle, he suddenly began to breathe more easily.

Allen checked his altimeter: 9,700 feet. He had reached the indifferent stage, where oxygen was 90–98 per cent. He kept taking long deep breaths, needing to get back to normality.

Massive shapes were growing out of the dark: the mountains of Badakhshan, the rocky heights that surrounded the LS.

Allen turned and looked over his shoulder and up. Through his NVGs he saw Banks about 30 metres away and up maybe another 10. Looking down at the valleys, there was no sign of life, or even of habitation. This was a wild land. No wonder the kidnappers had brought the hostages here.

With oxygen coursing through his body, Allen felt like a man reborn. Suddenly his senses were sharper. His muscles reacted instantly. He felt a flash of pride at how he'd responded to the crisis, but put that emotion away as quickly as he had done fear. There was still a long way to go.

The mountains were rising fast. Their final approach to their LS so they could land into the wind required passing over a ridge close enough to touch it. Any higher than that and they would overshoot and land in the thick forest beyond the clearing.

Allen braced himself as the mountainside loomed towards him. Night vision was not well suited to judging depth, and so Allen lifted the goggles up, making the decision that there was enough moonlight for him to see what was ahead of him. He looked at the moon itself, saw no clouds around it, and was confident it would not be obstructed behind clouds when he needed it most.

A rising thermal current lifted Allen up as it hit his canopy. It was the kind of jolt that would shake an inexperienced parachutist, but Allen corrected his course without needing to think.

The thick mountain ridge began to run beneath him, less than 10 metres beneath Allen's boots. For the first time since jumping, he became aware of his speed, and the ridge flashed by in a few seconds. The valley opened up before him, and at the end of it he saw the inviting space of the LS.

The fastest, most efficient way in was to ride down the valley like a ski lift, braking strongly in the final moments to drop into the clearing. It would be a hard landing, but a lot of military parachuting was. So long as he could walk away and do his job, bumps and bruises didn't matter. Allen had always been fascinated with the glider pilots who had crash-landed their aircraft in airborne operations in places like Normandy and Arnhem. That was how he felt now. That he was gliding in for a crash landing, and that once he did, the fight was just beginning.

As the sides of the valley rushed by, Allen pushed down on his hook release handles to unlock his bergen. The shoulder straps were around his thighs; the bergen fell away but was stopped from falling into the darkness by his boots. Beneath Allen's bergen was a thick canvas of trees. He flared the canopy to drop some speed and height, aware that if he lost too much too quickly he would pile into the forest before hitting the clearing. And the more height he lost, the harder the drop zone was to see. Allen realised that it was going to come up on him in a flash, and when it did, he would need to brake hard and fast. But he had a trick up his sleeve that was going to save him from totally crumbling into the ground.

Suddenly the trees thinned and the clearing appeared and Allen let the bergen fall from his boots and dangle below him via a three-metre rope. As soon as he heard the pack making contact with the ground, Allen pulled down slow and sharp on the toggles of his rigging and his canopy started to collapse. As the air rushed out of it, Allen fell as if jumping from a wall, landing momentarily on his feet, but he couldn't keep himself stable. He collapsed onto his arse, which hurt. Quickly he began to pull the parachute in to clear the area for Banks.

Allen told himself that the American had the benefit of seeing where he had landed, and that was why he touched down with the grace of an eagle, even releasing his bergen from his boots just before they made contact with the ground. There was no doubt that the SEAL was one of the best parachutists Allen had ever seen, but that didn't make him happy that he had lost his footing on landing while Banks had kept his.

Silently, the two men collapsed their rigs; they would be taking them to minimise compromise. On an OP job, everything you take in you take out, and that even includes your shit. Nothing must remain in the target area; if have to come back another time, you don't want it to be to an area that's been compromised. The most powerful weapon these two men had wasn't their firepower: it was concealment.

Allen pulled out his comms from the side pouch of his bergen as Banks checked out the ground for the Black Hawks. The ops room needed a sitrep (situation report), mainly to know that they were on the ground and in good order to move forward and that the air planners were correct, that the ground was good to insert the teams onto.

'On the ground and moving off in five.'

Banks knelt beside him and low-toned into his free ear. 'Dust.'

'The ground is good, it'll be a dust landing. Closing down now.'

'You good to go?' Allen asked Banks.

'Are you? Looked like you came in a little hot there.' The SEAL shouldered his kit and lifted his weapon into the low-ready with a smile. 'I didn't need to check out the HLS; your ass already knew the ground was hard enough.'

CHAPTER 37

Badakhshan Province covers a little over 44,000 square kilometres, a lot of it occupied by the Pamir and Hindu Kush mountain ranges. The province has 520 prominent mountains, the tallest of them being Kohe Shakawr, at 7,086m. Allen and Banks weren't climbing that peak, but their muscles were burning as they carried the burdens of their equipment up the steep trail that led from the LS to a ridge that they would need to cross if they wanted to descend into the next valley where the hostages were maybe being held. It was a difficult route, but the only one that worked. The only closer viable LS would have had them landing at the cave mouth, and that wasn't going to happen.

As Allen's sweat saturated all his clothing and dripped off his face he thought about the sad truth that these four women wouldn't be getting the attention of NATO if they had all been Afghans or even Kenyans. Their shitty situation was made just a little better because there was a Brit in the mix, which meant there was a possibility that the SF of two nations would rescue them.

A lot was riding on what Allen and Banks could discover on their recce. They might not be in the cave – then what? Perhaps they would be able to move the needle from 'impossible' to 'difficult' but that wouldn't guarantee the rest of their teams would attempt to release the hostages. That depended on people way up the food chain in London giving the go or no-go. The failed attempt in the Korengal had not only put SF operations in the spotlight, but these four women. Allen realised that no one really gave a shit about all four.

The men hit an altitude that made it too hard for the trees to survive and they were in open ground. Allen could feel the thin air, but after what he'd been through in his descent, it was no sweat. Like many of his days of service in the SAS, Allen's boundaries had been pushed and they'd moved.

He lifted his night vision and looked around him. They were climbing up a ridge that formed the end of the valley, the sides of which were steep and harsh. Beyond them, in the moonlight, he could see silhouettes of other mountain peaks. The whole area looked like something out of *The Lord of the Rings*. Allen wasn't one for movies but he'd made an exception when he learned that the books the movies were based on were written by a man who'd served in the trenches. The author had seen life at its worst. Humans, at their worst. But also at their best, too. What else was the relationship between the characters if not those of comrades of war? Those were stories that resonated with Allen.

CHAPTER 38

It took them three hours to climb the ridge and start dropping down into the next valley and towards the target cave. During that entire time Allen and Banks didn't speak a word to each other. There was no need. Banks had moved through the wooded mountainside like he had been born in it, and Allen grimaced whenever he set foot on a dry, snapping twig. The American was as silent as a ghost and that bothered Allen:

He's better at this than I am.

Being anything other than the best ate at Allen, but he forced himself to compartmentalise the feeling, knowing that to think about it would only affect him negatively, at least now. When this mission was done, Allen knew that the feeling of being second best would lead him to practise harder, to train for longer, but right now he was where he was, and so he tried to empty his mind of everything but the mission.

Banks halted short of a rocky escarpment and silently slid his kit from his shoulder before crawling out onto the rocks. Allen did the same, and followed. When he came beside the American, he was looking almost lengthways down into the valley. Most of it was covered in evergreen trees, but the heights of the valleys were bald and craggy.

The bottom of the valley was undulating and barren, the open area no wider than a football field. Allen could just about make out tracks worn into the dirt. It was far from a road, suitable only for 4x4s. In the winter, Allen reckoned that the pass would be closed off completely.

If they were here to keep eyes on the valley itself, then they were in a great position, but they had come to gather intelligence on the cave, and what was inside it. There was no way of doing that from here.

'We need to go lower,' Allen whispered.

Banks nodded, and began moving backwards. Moments later both men had reshouldered their kit, and were heading deeper into the valley.

It took another two hours to get to the height that they needed. This time, when Banks unburdened himself of equipment and crawled forward, Allen could see a dark shape in a cliff face: it was the cave entrance. He could see that, but nothing else.

Allen tapped Banks on the shoulder and gestured that they move back into more cover.

'We need to get closer,' he whispered when they were in better cover. 'We need to be able to see inside.'

'Not going to happen. To get as low as the cave we'll be out of the treeline, no cover.'

'Well we can't achieve much from here.'

'Agreed. We should set up an OP here to observe activity coming in or out, but we're going to need to do a close target recon. We need to get inside the cave.'

Allen wasn't sure he'd heard him correctly. 'You want to go inside?'

'We're not going to see shitloads of hostages from here, are we? How the fuck are we going to find out if they're connected to a tunnel? You see any other way of getting this done?'

Allen didn't. Still, something told him that what the American had in mind was reckless. 'If we fuck it up they'll kill the hostages.'

'So we don't fuck it up.'

'I'm just telling you what's at stake.'

'I know the risks. We doing this or not?'

Allen pulled back the cuff of his sleeve and looked at the luminescent hands. 'We've got two hours until first light. Let's get our sitrep out.'

'No, not yet,' Banks replied.

'You think they'll tell us to stay put ...'

'I think we're the ones on the ground and the call should be ours, not someone drinking coffee in an ops room. The drones will show 'em what we're doing anyway.'

Allen understood his reasoning. Better to ask forgiveness than permission, but there would be no forgiveness if they fucked this up. That was, if they even survived long enough to ask for it.

'All right, let's do it.'

'Agreed,' Allen replied. The less clutter the better. He knew what they were about to do was pushing the limits, even going beyond them, but it wasn't without precedent. In 2000, during Operation Barras, members of the SAS had rescued members of the Royal Irish Regiment being held captive in Sierra Leone by a group known as the West Side Boys. The night before the raid, a small team of the SAS had infiltrated the enemy's camp and let the hostages know that an assault was coming in the morning, and what to do when it did. Then there was the decades of covert work in Northern Ireland, working under the noses of the terrorists. SAS soldiers would go out alone, in plain clothes, and frequent hot spots of resistance. It was the kind of work that tested a man's mettle. 'Sneaky beaky', some called it. It was the kind of work that had no margin for error. One slip-up could mean capture, torture and a lonely death. It was the kind of high risk/high reward work that had thrilled Allen as a young man when he'd read about it. He wanted to do this – no doubt about it – but he wouldn't be a professional if he didn't consider the downside.

Allen ran through the pros and cons in his head. If they were seen, then they couldn't expect anything but failure, and death for the hostages. On the other hand, they were on the ground to confirm if the hostages were inside the cave. If they were, how many were protecting them and how? The sooner that was done the better for all concerned.

'Let's do it.'

CHAPTER 39

BAGRAM

One of Vasquez's analysts entered his smoke-filled office to hand him a typescript. He read it, then handed it to Powell. She read it once, read it twice, then handed it back to her American counterpart.

'Fuck.'

'Yep,' Vasquez agreed. 'You want to tell them?'

Powell nodded and left the room.

It was a short walk to the special forces compound. Powell knocked on the door of the SAS ops room. It was opened by Baz, the squadron sergeant major, who read her expression and frowned. 'Come in.'

Inside the ops room were a number of the regiments' officers and support specialists. All eyes turned her way. Powell wasted no time.

She pointed to the drone screen and the two heat signatures moving about the valley.

Baz nodded. 'So far all good. The team's standing by if it doesn't stay good and they need extraction.'

Powell looked around the room, making sure that she had everyone's full attention. She had that, and more. 'Thirty minutes ago, we intercepted a call that triangulated to the target area, so that heightens the possibility the hostages are in that cave.

'The bad news is that the call was to express their frustration at how long the Afghan government are taking to meet their demands. The kidnappers have asked their leadership for permission to make a show of intent.'

A couple of the people inside the ops room groaned. Most just narrowed their eyes and looked angry.

Everyone knew what that meant. Anything from rape, digits, ears or noses cut away from their bodies, or one of them, probably an Afghan that not even they cared about, executed.

'And what was the answer?' one of the officers asked.

'So far there hasn't been one,' Powell told him. 'They've been told to wait for instruction.'

'What's the location of this leadership?' the officer asked. 'Maybe we could scoop him up, then use him for leverage. What's his position?'

'He is the local warlord in Fayzabad. He has more than a hundred fighters on his books. It would be a bigger op than this.'

'A Spectre gunship and Apaches would even the odds a bit,' Baz said.

'I'm sure they would.' Powell half laughed with her agreement because she often had the same thought about a lot of the operations she had been part of. 'But right now this warlord has stayed out of the war. So has most of the region. This guy just wants his cut of the cash for letting the kidnapping happen on his turf. At the very least we could expect the warlord's remaining men, and those of his clan, to join the Taliban.'

'How active are they in the area?' an officer asked her.

'They have a presence, but they don't have the same kind of footprint as they do in Helmand, for instance.'

'Could they make a play for the hostages?'

Powell considered her answer. 'If there's one thing we've learned about the Taliban, it's that they never walk away from an opportunity and we shouldn't put anything past them.'

She turned back to the drone screen and watched the two heat signatures slowly moving about the target area with no indication of what the OP team had planned.

CHAPTER 40

Allen and Banks cached their equipment, which they covered with cam netting and branches, and then slipped lower into the valley.

They wore just their plate carriers and helmets, with NVGs attached, and for weapons they carried only sidearms and blades. They needed ease of movement, and less kit also meant less noise. In any event, if it went noisy they would have really fucked up, and being fully bombed-up wasn't going to help them that much at all.

Allen carried a Fairbairn-Sykes fighting knife which had been gifted to him following a series of combined operations with the Royal Marines. Fairbairn and Sykes designed the double-bladed knife for the Shanghai Police Force in the 1930s and the design turned out to be so perfect it was still being used 80 years later. He liked the blade for its simple, graceful design which gave both a sharp stabbing point and two cutting edges. Tearing into an artery cannot guarantee a silent kill as a torn artery will contract – it is nature's attempt to stop the bleeding – so the target is still breathing and makes noise. But a clean cut from a Fairbairn-Sykes keeps the target's breathing time to a minimum.

Banks's blade of choice was a little more audacious: a tomahawk, like those carried by Native American tribes, and later by the irregular forces who had fought against the Redcoats in what Allen knew as the American War of Independence, and what Banks would have been taught at school as the Revolutionary War. It was a brutal instrument, and a favourite with US special operations forces. Allen thought that part of the reason was because it 'looked cool', but the Tomahawk also had its practical uses, much like a machete. It could be used for breaking locks, and Allen had also heard of it being used to retrieve pieces of dead terrorists' melted and destroyed bodies so that they could be positively ID'd.

Though the suppressed pistols in their hands were far more deadly, there was something about a blade that inspired fear in a man's heart. It was one thing to pull a trigger, particularly at a distance. It was another to be so close to a man that you could feel his breath before plunging cold steel into him. Allen had never killed anyone that way, and if this recce went as planned, he wouldn't have to. Their objective was to get in and out unseen.

Once again, Allen couldn't help but be impressed by how Banks moved. He was a big guy but he ghosted his way through the trees. Allen didn't know, and he wasn't going to ask, but his guess was that, like many Americans in special operations, Banks had grown up hunting. That culture was a big part of life where many of them had spent their early years, and blooding from their first kill was seen as a rite of passage. It was no wonder that America produced such good snipers, and hunters of men. Deer, wolves and bears were a lot harder to stalk than the average human being. Their sense of smell, sight and hearing were far superior. Hunting game required a man to learn how to mask his movements. It taught patience and tact. For most British soldiers, the first life that they ever took was that of another person. For many Americans, they had learned to control their breathing and master adrenaline from an early age. Allen thought that this spoke highly as to how effective British Army training was. Britain's soldiers were as good as any in the world, and its special forces were arguably the gold standard. They might not have been raised hunting, but they mastered it all the same.

Seeing Banks move, Allen realised how much there was to learn from people who had spent their lives stalking. Much of a soldier's training was done at full speed, and for good reason – assaulting a position or building required speed, aggression and violence of action – but there was another part to soldiering that required the opposite – a cool, calm, methodical approach.

Snipers were known for their patience, but the truth was that every soldier must learn the same if they were ever to be masters of their profession. In the jungles of Brunei, it had taken thousands of hours of patrolling for every one enemy killed. It was not the hard, fast, direct action that had become common in the Global War on Terror but something more primal, no different from when man had been living as hunters and gatherers. One mistake, one loss of patience, and those thousands of hours of patrolling could be wasted. Tonight, Allen was walking in the footsteps of his ancestors, both ancient and regimental. He had to put his bread and butter of door kicking and violence from his mind, and become a silent, stalking hunter, where his prize was intelligence and the location of the hostages.

Banks came to a stop as they reached the edge of the wooded hillside and knelt down beside a tree. Allen stopped a few metres to the American's right and provided security while Banks lifted his night-vision goggles away from his face and raised a monocular sight to his eye. The device had thermal vision, and Banks slowly swept the terrain in front of them, looking for heat signatures. When he lowered the device he raised his hand and held up two fingers, then turned his thumb downwards: two armed enemy.

Allen didn't know how Banks planned on getting by them, but he had seen enough of the man's stealth to trust that if anyone could slip by two guards, it was this SEAL. And he didn't doubt his own ability either, because if one man could do it, then so could he. That had always been Allen's attitude to life. If someone else could do it, then why not him? There was a thin line between confidence and hubris, but Allen knew that his superiors saw the same in him. They wouldn't have sent him if they didn't trust him to get the job done.

Allen pulled back his sleeve and looked at his watch. They had little over an hour to spend on target, then they would need to withdraw so that they weren't moving at first light. Even with the cover from the forest, movement could be spotted, particularly in a place like this where there was so little movement and noise. They were cutting it fine, but it was the only way to cut it. They had the opportunity to find out if these hostages were really inside the cave, and that was what they were going to do.

Banks pulled his goggles back down into place and moved off at a crouch. He moved left, back into the trees, and followed them for almost a hundred metres before he then changed direction into the open ground. He read the folds in the ground like the pages of a book, giving himself and Allen every bit of cover available. Their upper bodies were still exposed, but Banks was working on the calculated assumption that being inside the cave mouth severely restricted the sentries' fields of vision. By standing inside the cave they had shielded themselves from the cameras of the circling American drones, out of sight and sound, but in doing so they had limited themselves to seeing only what was in front of the cave mouth. And so, Banks led them in from the left flank.

They held tight to the steep mountainside in which the cave was housed. Allen's heart was trying to thump with nervous excitement but he willed it to be still. He left his mouth slightly open to improve his hearing, and his nose wrinkled as he smelt the unmistakable scent of burning wood. During the jungle phase of SAS selection, Allen had learned just how powerful a human's sense of smell could be. In daily life people are bombarded by so many smells that it becomes overwhelming, and usually blend together to become unnoticeable through overload. Not so in nature. In nature, a person can detect smoke and other odours that stand out from the natural world from an incredible distance. Scent was something of a lost art, but the expert trackers had taught Allen and his ilk how to use it to their advantage. A special forces soldier must look for an edge. Sometimes that meant the weapons he carried. Other times, it was the senses that he had been given at birth but never realised to their full potential.

Banks led the way as they stalked towards the cave mouth. Allen became aware of the low, tired chatter of two men. He didn't understand the words but the tone was universal: the men were bored. Being on stag (guard duty) tested the patience of soldiers the world over, and these men were no different. They should have been silent and alert, listening for any sounds in the valley. Instead, they were trying to make their time on watch go faster by talking to each other. Maybe about what they'd spend their share of the ransom on, or about their children, or about God. There was no end of things that men would talk about in the early hours when they were bored to their core.

For Allen, this mumbling of boredom while on stag meant that yes, there was more than just one face picked up by the drone. But all that was certain was that there were two. But the fact that they were stagging on indicated they were protecting something, but that of course could be themselves.

Banks held up a hand for Allen to stop, and then put two fingers towards his eyes. Banks slowly crawled closer to the mouth of the cave.

Allen crept forward behind him until he was in a better position, with eyes on Banks to cover him as he got closer to the dark hole that contained the bored murmurs. For what seemed like an eternity, Banks lay still just a metre short of the cave mouth, listening for anything that could give him the information they needed.

Eventually Banks started to back out of his position, and only after a couple of metres did he turn to face Allen as he continued his crawl back to his team member.

Both men made more distance from the cave before Banks leaned in to Allen, the two men's heads so close they could feel each other's breath.

Banks spoke gently in a low tone. Whispering can sometimes be louder and more difficult to understand, which just means more time making noise.

'The sentries are slack and anyone else in there is probably asleep. I couldn't hear anything else.'

Allen sensed an opportunity.

'We can drop them and be inside before they even know we're there – and if they're inside, get them out, now.'

The SEAL grasped his meaning and whispered back. 'You want to take them?'

'Why not? We're here, they're slack and maybe, if they *are* in there, we can get the hostages and be away before first light.

There was a pause before Banks replied. The petty officer was weighing up the pros and cons. 'No,' he said at last.

'Look, we can't get into the cave if those two fucks are breathing, so we can't find out if they're inside or not. But if we drop the stag, we crack on and maybe get the four of them out, right now. We can do it.'

'I know we can do it. I'm saying we're not going to.'

'Why?'

'Because that wasn't our fucking mission. We're here to gather intel, not go Jack Ryan. We stick to the plan.'

Allen had different views on that, and it was the Korengal events that had formed them so deeply into his brain. 'The best that we can do is rescue the fucking hostages. No more dead ones, yeah?'

Banks was about to say more, but it was too late.

In the caves, someone was shouting.

CHAPTER 41

Umid was shaken from sleep and blinked against the lights inside of the cave. He was tired, dog tired, but Daler was standing over him with a big smile on his face.

'Get up. We have work to do.'

Umid was too tired and confused to ask questions. Instead, he pushed himself onto his weary feet. It felt like only two minutes since he'd come off watch and closed his eyes. He rolled his shoulders. The thin blanket he had wrapped around him didn't make for much comfort on the hard cave floors.

Looking around, Umid saw that the other bandits were also getting to their feet, some of them talking quietly among themselves. Like Daler, a few were smiling.

'Come on,' Daler said. 'Sherali is waiting.'

Umid followed on out of the cave chamber that served as the men's sleeping quarters. He found the rest of the men standing outside the small cavern that was used to house 'the guests'.

When Umid looked at Sherali, he saw a new face on the man. The perennial, wry smile that seemed to always be on the old bandit's face was gone. Instead, he looked as grim and sombre as winter.

'Umid,' Sherali said, 'take this.'

He pulled a battered old Russian Tokarev pistol from his belt and handed it to the dazed young man.

CHAPTER 42

BAGRAM

Rachael Powell ran into the SAS's ops room with such force that she almost took the door off its hinges. The room's half-dozen occupants swung around to face her.

'What's happened?' the sergeant major asked.

'The kidnapper's received a call,' she said, mastering her breathing and not allowing her sprint between the compounds to affect the delivery of her message. 'They told them to give one of the hostages the same treatment as they did to Abdul.'

'Who the fuck is Abdul?' Baz asked.

'We don't know. But this isn't good. We're running down past cases and reports to try and find someone who matches that name, and this situation, but it's unlikely we'll find anything. It's such a common name and besides, most Afghan on Afghan kidnappings are never reported, at least not to us.'

'What do you think it means?' the SSM asked her.

'Two things,' Powell replied. 'That the person on the phone is smart enough to know that they may be getting listened in. And that they're about to make some kind of statement with the hostages.'

The sergeant major clenched his jaw, then Baz asked what everyone was thinking.

'What kind?'

'Boss,' one of the regimental support staff said, turning Baz's attention away from Powell. 'There's movement outside of the caves. Two heat signatures.'

Powell and Baz looked at each other, and then walked quickly over to the footage that was being relayed by the Predator drone. From the way that the figures were moving, it could only be two men.

Allen and Banks.

CHAPTER 43

Umid watched as the four hostages were dragged out of their quarters and into the larger cave chamber. He couldn't think of them as guests, now, not as they were being dragged screaming by their hair.

Is this real? he asked himself. It felt like he was still dreaming. A few minutes ago he had been dead asleep, and now his body was shaking with nerves. His mouth was dry. He was aware of a distant ringing in his ears. In moments, he had gone from peace, to ... this. He still wasn't sure what this was, but he knew it was different, and dangerous. He could smell it. He could smell the women's fear.

Adele was shouting in a language he could not understand, but he understood the terror in it. Tasneem's words were a lot clearer.

'Let go of me! How dare you! You are not my family! Not my husband! How dare you lay a hand on me!'

Daler replied by slapping her hard across the face. Tasneem looked at him defiantly.

'Only witches are not afraid!'

Daler hit her harder.

Umid's stomach knotted. He had grown up in a place where violence towards women was normal, but something was different now. He had the sickening feeling that it would not end with a simple beating but something more final. Something that he would be asked to do.

Why else had Sherali given him a pistol? Why else would the other bandits be watching him, and smiling, and saying things quietly to each other that Umid could not hear.

'Here will do,' Sherali said, and the four hostages were kicked and pulled onto their knees. Umid looked at their faces. On some he saw fear. Others had vacant eyes, like their souls had fled ahead of the terror of the moment. Umid felt a rising tide of bile in his throat. He was scared, too. Scared that he would show weakness. Scared that he would fail this test.

'Start recording,' Sherali told one of the bandits, and the man held up the mobile phone. Sherali wrapped the end of his turban around his face, then stepped into view before the four kneeling hostages.

The younger Afghan aid worker, Zahab, felt Sherali's hand on her shoulder from behind. Umid watched transfixed as she began to shake violently at the thought of what was about to happen.

'Our demands were clear,' he spoke towards the recording bandit. 'We told you how much, and we told you to release our brother, Jallah. Neither of our demands have been met.'

'Please, no,' the young woman whimpered. 'Please, be merciful.'

Zahab started to pray out loud in a desperate attempt to talk to God before she met him.

Sherali's eyes were on Umid. 'Cover your face.'

Umid couldn't move his hands to do as he had been told.

'Come!'

Umid's feet were cemented to the floor. He felt like his body belonged to another person. Daler stepped towards him, wrapped a cloth around Umid's face, and then pushed him forward. Umid almost stumbled into the camera's view. He stood before the young Afghan woman. She saw the pistol in his hand and gave an almost animal moan of terror.

'Not her,' Sherali said. 'This one.'

Umid followed the pointing finger...

Tasneem.

The older woman stared defiantly at him as Zahab passed out and slumped into the dust.

There was no hint of fear in Tasneem's eyes. Umid had felt that stare before, when his mother had been disappointed in him. Daler stepped forward and punched her in the face to wipe away her indignation and judgement.

Umid raised the pistol higher and pointed it at Tasneem's face.

'Become a man,' Daler told him. 'Do it!'

CHAPTER 44

For a moment Allen thought that the shouts from within the cave must have meant they'd been spotted, and he'd raised his pistol into the aim, but no one came out to look for him. After a moment, he realised that the shouts had the unmistakable sound of fear: it wasn't the stag shouting.

Allen and Banks wasted no time, ghosting towards the entrance. The stag was gone.

Banks turned back and looked at Allen. He saw the glowing eyes of the NVGs looking back at him. Allen gave a single nod.

Go.

They fanned out on either side of the cave mouth. Something was blocking the rear of the cave. Dull light tried hard to push past, its weak and yellow glow slipping between the gaps. It was flat, like a wall, about 10 metres deeper inside the cave. It took a second or two for Banks and Allen to work out that blankets had been hung to keep out the lights of the interior. In among the shouting beyond the blankets, he could hear the chug of a diesel generator. He could smell it.

Allen and Banks looked at one another. Banks motioned his hand towards the ground: go firm. Don't move.

Allen knew that this was the right thing to do. Beyond the blankets were two Afghan females and one that was definitely African. One more to go and they would have achieved what they'd been sent to do.

If they moved forward now that everyone was no longer sleeping and tried a rescue it would mean a fight, with the hostages caught in the middle.

But they still had to confirm if Laura, the Brit, was with the other three. Her voice should be easy to distinguish over the begs, sobbing and excitement beyond the blankets, but still the two men heard nothing from her.

Allen pushed his NVGs up, then started moving slowly towards the blankets. He didn't have to say anything to Banks. He would cover his movement. Allen gently pulled back the curtain, just enough to see into the smoke-hazed cave.

Four women's faces – two Afghan, one black, one white – were in a line and were on their knees. Around them were a dozen armed men. Most were smoking and smiling, excited about what was going to happen. But Allen picked up something about these hostage-takers that only a trained eye would notice. These men might be enjoying themselves, but every man's safety lever on their weapon was at safe. The lighting made the gun oil on their weapons glint just enough to indicate there were soldiering skills among the group. They had the discipline, or were being disciplined, to keep their weapons' working parts in good order.

Allen could feel the weight of the pistol in his hand. It was a battle against his instinct not to raise it, and start firing, but it would be futile. There was no way of taking out all of them before all the hostages would be killed in the crossfire. He had to stand firm. To watch.

An older man stood behind the younger Afghan women and started to speak at a bandit holding a camera. Allen dared to hope. If they were recording this, maybe it was another ransom demand. Maybe that's all this was.

And then a young bandit was pushed forward towards them with a pistol in his hands. Allen knew then that death was moments away. And then, he was forced to make a decision. If they were all about to be executed, he and Banks would have to take action no matter the risk. And that was even greater now, knowing that these men were disciplined and trained.

Allen had to be sure before he took action that these women were definitely about to be killed, or would be before an attack could go in and rescue them. He would wait until the first woman fell to the ground and then move in. Three saved was better than none: that was what he told himself. But that didn't make watching any easier.

Not easier at all. It would be a total gangfuck, but there would be no other way of getting the other three out of the cave alive.

The bandit with the pistol stopped in front of the younger Afghan woman. She was praying, still shaking violently with nerves. Allen was aware of a sick feeling in his stomach, but he pushed it away. He had to be ready. The other three women just stared at the ground, waiting for the death of their friend, deep in thought. Chances were, they would be next. Allen remained a pair of eyes, taking in every bit of information that he could – information that could mean the lives of the other hostages. Who would he drop first? It would be the executor: his weapon was already in his hand. After that it would be any target that was in front of him. It would be all about getting rounds into bodies as fast as he could.

The bandit with the pistol stepped away from the shaking Afghan woman, who passed out and slumped to the floor. Now he stood in front of the older Afghan. She showed no fear. Her bravery made Allen want to act more than ever.

Instead, he watched as the bandit raised his pistol, pointed it at her face, and pulled the trigger.

CHAPTER 45

The pistol's hammer thumped forward.

Click.

Tasneem, still alive and full of power, stared back at Umid. She hadn't blinked once. It took Umid a moment to realise that the pistol that he held in shaking hands had misfired. That was all it took for Allen to look back to confirm Banks was behind him before pushing into the light.

He stopped as an old voice shouted out beyond the blanket.

'Enough!' Sherali looked towards the camera. 'Next time, there will be a bullet in there for her,' he declared, 'and one less woman can go home. You know our demands. Meet them. There will not be a second chance.'

Allen watched as the old Afghan nodded at the cameraman to stop filming and then thunderous laughter filled the cave.

Daler laughed, slapping Umid on the shoulder. 'You are now a man.'

Umid didn't feel like one as the four prisoners were hauled to their feet and taken back to their chamber.

'You two,' Sherali said to a pair of bandits, 'get back on guard. Umid, my pistol.'

Umid handed it over. Sherali unloaded the empty magazine from the Tokayev, and pushed in its replacement, fully loaded with eight rounds and made ready, all in moments.

'You did well,' Sherali told him. 'You never know if you can really count on a man until he has killed for you, and you did that, or as close to it that matters.'

'Why?' Umid found himself asking.

'For you? To earn your place. For the camera, to put fear in their hearts. Now their eyes have been opened to what can be. They know that next time it will be real.'

'I still think we should have killed one,' Daler said. 'That would send a strong message.'

'You've been to a market, Daler. If you want to buy four melons, and the shopkeeper smashes one, would you still pay for it?'

'That is assuming they value these women equally,' Daler replied, 'which they do not. If they cared about Afghan lives they wouldn't be fighting their war here. We only need the white woman. Maybe the black one too. But the Afghan women are disposable.'

Sherali smiled and shook his head. 'You're quick to say they don't value Afghan lives, but you would condemn two to death just to make a point.'

Daler thought about that for a moment, then nodded. 'We're bandits, not doctors.'

'Indeed.' Sherali nodded, too. 'Get some rest, Umid. And well done.'

Umid walked away and lay on his thin blanket. He knew that he could not sleep. Indeed, he wondered if he would ever sleep again.

CHAPTER 46

Allen and Banks had almost moved back as far as the mouth of the cave by the time the laughter started. There was a high possibility the stag would return. They had reached their cached equipment just as the sky was turning from black to grey. First light had come. They had little time to position and camouflage themselves for the coming day, but little time was all they needed. Instead of digging in, they found a fold in the ground on the mountainside. Using fallen branches they fashioned a structure that looked natural, but which could bear camouflage netting. They didn't use a thermal blanket to hide their heat signatures. After getting a good look at the bandits, it had appeared they had very little in the way of technology. There were lights in the cave powered by a diesel generator, but there had been no sign of any optics on the men's weapons, which were predominantly old and well-used AK-47s.

As Allen nestled into the observation post, he suddenly felt weary to his bones. It had been a long night. The jump had been a mental and physical battle. The insertion from the LS to the cave had been hard going over the mountainside. He was exhausted. From the look of Banks, he felt the same way. The SEAL's usual vigour had been dampened. Only a robot could see something like that and not experience a flood of adrenaline. When that wore off, all that was left was fatigue.

They settled into their OP position with the satisfaction of knowing that the hostages had been confirmed and so a plan of action could be put forward for the go or no-go.

CHAPTER 47

Allen talked slowly into the sat phone as he gave the ops room the OP team's sitrep.

'All four are on target. They look mostly unharmed and able to walk.'

There was a pause while Baz allowed Allen's details to be written on the log sheet of what they had seen and heard.

'No other exit was seen in the cave, just one way in and out.'

'Roger.'

'We have a start line for the assault team and a heli exfil will be good outside the cave.'

'Roger that. Keep eyes on.'

'How long before the go/no-go?'

'On it now. We'll push for it one way or another. Out.'

Allen placed the sat phone down.

Banks was on stag, his eyes fixed on the cave's entrance. 'And?'

'Keep eyes on and we wait. I'll take the first watch. You look like shit.'

CHAPTER 48

BAGRAM

Powell and Vasquez looked across the conference table at the US Commander, NATO Forces Afghanistan, the British Ambassador to Afghanistan, and the UK's Oversight Committee.

'Where are we with the ransom demands?' the NATO commander asked the assembly.

'The Afghan government is still stalling them for us,' the ambassador replied. The lean man wore a dark suit and a dark expression. He had come to Kabul to help build a country, but found himself frequently involved in emergency repairs instead.

The American general leaned towards his 2i/c. 'What's the situation on the ground?'

'We have an OP with eyes on and have confirmation that all four hostages are alive and inside the cave. A little roughed up, but no sign of serious injury.'

'And the cave?' The commander's eyes remained fixed on his 2i/c, the only person in the room he knew and trusted. 'Are we talking Tora Bora, or just a hole in the wall?' Tora Bora were the infamous labyrinth of caves in which Osama bin Laden had been cornered, yet somehow escaped from, in 2001. It had been the site of a massive, bloody battle.

'All the imagery, plus what the OP has seen, indicates there is just the one entry point some four metres wide. The main cavern is some 40 metres deep and branches off into several smaller chambers.' He pushed a sketch towards his boss and tapped it with his pen. 'The hostages were seen there.' He tapped the drawing with his pen. 'Behind that line, it's a curtain of blankets.'

'They went inside? A real close target recce?'

'Yes, sir.'

The commander raised half a smile. 'Good skills.'

'Yes, sir. A UK–US OP team.'

The commander got back to work.

'What do we know about the kidnappers?'

He pushed the sketch back towards his 2i/c but now changed his focus.

'The OP counted 12, all armed. There is an element of discipline, at least to a degree we don't always see in this country. There are almost always two men on guard just inside the cave mouth.' His head turned in Vasquez's direction. 'Is this one of your lot, Fede? Did the company train these guys up?'

Vasquez shrugged. 'It's possible, sir. At least some of them. When we first came into this country, shortly after 9/11, it was a special forces and clandestine operation. Green Berets did what they do best, and worked with partner forces from the local population. The north of the country has never really been friendly with the Taliban, and before that they fought hard against the Russians.'

'So what you're saying is that those weapons they're carrying were paid for by Uncle Sam?'

'It's very possible, sir. And it's possible that some of the kidnappers were trained in the early days of the war before the Taliban fell.'

'By the CIA?'

'By the company, sir, yes.'

The general sighed to himself. 'Enemies become allies, allies become enemies. That's how it's always been in this part of the world, I suppose, so no point getting upset about it.'

The former director of UKSF agreed and wanted to get back to the here and now. 'If it goes noisy and we need the Emergency Response, it's 30 minutes' Black Hawk time from Fayzabad to target. We can have the teams in the air in less than 10. The downside of the ER is that the only quick-time LS is outside the cave, giving the kidnappers warning and so time to do something irreversible.'

Powell liked his choice of words. It seemed a lot more pleasant than saying 'murder the hostages'.

The 2i/c let that sink in for a second before continuing.

'But, we know the hostages are in the cave, we have eyes on the only exit, we have air assets giving us surveillance of the surrounding area. We are in an ideal situation to plan a Deliberate Response.'

The general thought about it for a long moment. 'As much as I want to smack down these bastards, I don't want to waste the lives of good men if money can get the job done.' He looked at the British ambassador who was in agreement. 'I think maybe it's time you spoke again with Number 10. Let's get this thing over and done with as soon as we can.'

CHAPTER 49

FOB FAYZABAD, BADAKHSHAN

Miller and Taff sat beside each other during the briefing update. The plan for the ER really was just to get in on the target as quickly as possible, smash whatever was in the way and grab the hostages. That was because information was at a minimum. As more intelligence became available, the ER plan would be updated. At the same time, a Deliberate Option, a plan in greater detail, was formulated. It entailed a more covert operation to get on target and attack without anyone in the cave being aware the teams were there – until the flash-bangs and assaulters came storming through the cave entrance. Only then would the plan have the three core values of an attack: speed, surprise and violence of action.

The two operators weren't the only SAS trooper and SEAL to have formed a friendship. The level of mutual respect between the units was high. Both units were elite and always looking for an edge. What was a wrinkle the other unit was using that they could incorporate into their own tactics? What had worked on previous missions? What had failed? Such cooperation, and the constant pursuit of excellence, was how the best of the best kept getting better. Never relax. Always refine. And, if necessary, tear it all up and start again.

Miller wondered what had happened to Allen and Banks. And so he wasn't that shocked when Coates walked to the front of the briefing room with a big smile on his face, and made his announcement.

'Okay, listen in, update. A two-man team, you know who they are, carried out a HAHO insertion onto the target and carried out a CTR of the cave.'

There was a wave of chatter and looks between the men, and a few muttered 'jammy bastards'. That was the kind of insertion that every SAS trooper and SEAL wanted to make.

'That's fucking ally.' Corporal Pritchard grinned. In the British army 'ally' was high praise indeed.

'I'll run you through the CTR details in a moment,' Coates told them, 'but first I just want to make you aware of something so you hear it from me first, and not a back channel. NATO will recommend to Number 10 a negotiated release.'

A ripple of groans went through the room.

'I know, I know, we all want to do this, but let's remember that the priority here is the lives of the hostages. If this is a no-go, we'll be back to doing direct action missions as soon as the OP team are withdrawn and the ER stood down.'

'Do we know when this meeting is, boss?' Taff asked.

'This is a priority for both sides right now, so I don't think we'll be waiting long for an answer. Either way, until Allen and Banks are off the ground we'll continue with the ER, still bombed-up and ready. If anything goes pear-shaped, we'll be the ones to pull them out. Any questions?'

A SEAL put his hand up.

'Yes?'

'What the fuck is a pear-shaped?'

Coates smiled. 'A snafu. Fubar. Not very good.'

'Understood. Thanks.'

'Any more? Yes, Taff?'

'How come we weren't told what Allen was doing before, boss?'

'Op Sec.'

Miller filled in the blanks: if things had gone badly, HQ would have withheld the news from everyone involved so as not to distract the politicians from their only requirement, to give the go and not the no-go. It was a hard tactic, but Miller could see the wisdom in it. So, by the grudging looks on their faces, did the other men in the room.

'Now, let's get into the details of what they found out on the recce ...'

CHAPTER 50

KABUL

Powell was once more sitting in the secure comms 'basement' in the British Embassy on her second satlink with Number 10. More than 3,000 miles away, in London, the faceless bureaucrat was yet again sitting in front of the stark white wall listening to the 2i/c of NATO Forces, Afghanistan.

'... and so, the general recommends that we pursue the avenue of negotiation. I'm sure the Afghan government will start negotiations for us. After all, that's whom the hostage-takers contacted.'

The bureaucrat looked unmoved. 'Britain, no matter what channels are used, does not negotiate with terrorists.'

'That's true,' the 2i/c replied, though everyone on the call knew that Britain did indeed negotiate with terrorists. The Good Friday Agreement was proof enough of that. Everyone taking part in the meeting knew that the Taliban would soon be opening an office in Qatar with the support of the US administration. Washington needed a neutral place to negotiate with the Islamist militia to prepare the withdrawal of troops from Afghanistan.

'... but these kidnappers have no affiliation to terrorist groups. And, as I'm sure you are well aware, even the Taliban themselves are not designated as a terrorist group, and we have negotiated with them in the recent past, when it has been prudent.'

The bureaucrat frowned. 'You're referring to Musa Qala?'

'Indeed.'

There had been negotiations with the Taliban that enabled the withdrawal of a rifle company of 16 Air Assault Brigade to prevent further destruction to the town.

'Correct me if I'm wrong, but didn't the Taliban then break their word and enter the town? And our forces had to launch a costly operation to push them out?'

'That is correct.'

'So all that negotiation bought was time, and then the same result. I feel that we would be inviting the same scenario here. Yes, we could pay the ransom and release their man, but what then? It would just send a message that if you kidnap a British civilian, Britain will reward you. We would be ending one kidnapping and inviting dozens more.'

'The general is aware of the possibility. However, this operation could prove costly, both in casualties and political capital, if it is unsuccessful. As far as hostage rescues go, this is about as difficult as it gets.'

The bureaucrat nodded. 'Difficult ... but not impossible?'

'Not impossible, no.'

'So what's your opinion?'

The former SAS officer smiled. 'My opinion? Let slip.'

Powell smiled to herself. *Let slip the dogs of war.*

The bureaucrat liked the sound of that himself. 'This government does not want to show weakness, however the prime minister has more than the situation on the ground to consider. I will convey your thoughts to him. For now, please remain planned and prepared.'

CHAPTER 51

Umid sat cross-legged with his AK-47 disassembled in his lap. Sherali insisted that his men clean their weapons daily. He would inspect them at random, and God help the man who had slacked in the care of his instrument.

'The cleanliness of this weapon means more than your life!' Sherali would berate them. 'It means the life of your brothers! Are you so lazy that you would let your brothers die? What does that say about you? Are you a man or a child? Then act like it! And if you can't, leave! The world will always need goat herders.'

So far Umid had escaped one of Sherali's tongue lashings, and he aimed to keep things that way. He cleaned his weapon twice a day, just to make sure. Daler noticed that and grinned slyly.

'You want to be his favourite.'

'No.'

'Don't worry, he already likes you. You did well this morning, Umid. Other men have failed that test. Not everyone is suited to this life. Some men are born to work in fields, others to carry a gun, and fewer still to use it. Everyone around you here has passed a similar test, though most did it with a firing pin in the weapon.'

'Did you?'

'Of course. It was five years ago, and a day I will never forget, of course. There was a shopkeeper. He hadn't been paying our boss what he was due, which was bad enough, but then we learned that he had been paying a rival instead. We had to make an example of him.'

Umid hoped that Daler stopped there, but the bandit seemed to be enjoying the story. 'He begged for his life, of course. He offered money. He even offered us his daughters. There was no honour in him, not a drop of loyalty. If he would sell his own family what would he do to us? He could not be trusted.

'I had only been with the boss for a short time, and so I didn't expect to be given the order to do it myself. Now, of course, I understand that it was a test of me, just as you were tested this morning. But they didn't give me a gun, Umid. They gave me a blade, and not a sharp one. It took a long time and a lot of effort to get his head from his shoulders. He squirmed like a worm and I kept losing my grip with the blood. The others were laughing at me. I was too embarrassed to be scared. When it was done we placed his head on the shelf, along with the goods that now belonged to us. After that I washed in a river. I had to buy new clothes. The blood would not come out, but I had earned my place.'

'What happened to his girls?' Umid found himself asking against his will.

'We took them, of course. They belonged to the boss, now. He sold them, I think.'

'To who?'

'What does it matter? They were his property, to do with as he wished. Remember that. Those women in there, they are not your family. They are the boss's property. If we are told to sell them, we sell them. If we are told to kill them, we kill them. It is as simple as that.'

Umid said nothing.

'This is your first time away from your family?' Daler asked, and Umid nodded.

'Then it is natural that you look for comfort, but your comfort is to be found with your brothers, and nowhere else. Do you understand?'

'I do,' said Umid, and he did. It was a hard lesson, but the world was hard.

'Sherali is not a cruel man, as some are. Some people kill for fun. Sherali only kills when it is necessary. Take comfort in that too.'

'I will.'

Daler smiled. 'You're a man now, Umid. You'll be a great man if you learn from Sherali. When we die, we will be judged on our loyalty to God, and to our patrons, and to our clan. Never forget that.'

He ruffled Umid's hair, then stood. 'Put that back together. It's our turn to watch the women.'

Umid reassembled his AK-47 with clumsy hands. He could still not strip it blindfolded like the other men could. He would in time, he told himself. He wanted to earn his place. This was his home now, and these were his brothers.

But that didn't make it any easier when he had to stand in front of the woman he had meant to kill. She didn't stare at him. Tasneem didn't even look at him at all. Before she had been friendly. She had seen her son in him. What did she see now?

A killer. A bandit.

Daler noticed Umid's discomfort and laughed. 'Now you are truly one of us.'

CHAPTER 52

BAGRAM

Federico Vasquez looked up from a sheaf of papers as his British counterpart entered his office.

'What have you got there?' she asked him.

'All in good time. How'd your satlink go?'

'Good, I suppose. No negotiations but still a no-go, but he liked the idea.'

'Okay. So why the suppose?'

Powell hesitated before answering. 'I think if we can get the hostages back without losing lives, maybe that's the smart play.'

'The problem with not risking any loss of life on our side is that it means we can't take any on theirs.'

'Sure, if this was a direct action, but it's supposed to be a rescue.'

Vasquez smiled. 'Is it? Hostage rescues aren't about saving lives. They're about sending warnings. Fuck with us, and we'll fuck you up.'

'That's pretty cynical, Fede. Even for a company guy.'

'Is it? Look how much this operation is costing. Teams of analysts. Teams of special forces. Black Hawks. Apaches. Predators. We're running in the millions upon millions.'

'You think?'

'Let's say the Brit was actually a really ill person back in the UK. Would she be getting all these resources to save her life?' Powell knew where he was heading with this.

'Well I'll tell you that in the US she'd be dead as fuck. But look at the effort we're putting in here. We're even willing to risk the lives of our operators, men who have received millions in training budget alone. I hate to be a dick, Rachael, but this isn't about the hostages. It's about power. Prestige. Showing the world that no one fucks with us. No one.'

'Is that all it is to you?'

'No. I want these women out alive. All of them. I'm just telling you what the big picture is.'

'I don't think the world's what it pretends to be, Fede. I wouldn't be here if I did.'

'Okay then. Good. Now are you ready for some good news?'

'I think I could use it after your inspiring pep talk, don't you?'

The American smiled. 'Our guys cleaned up the video audio and cross-checked all cell traffic in the last five years for any audio connection.'

Vasquez stopped for a dramatic pause but got nothing back from Powell. She had known him far too long.

'Sherali, that's the leader of those fucks in the cave. Sherali.'

Powell waited for more but the name meant nothing to her.

Vasquez pushed papers in front of him over to Powell. 'I'd heard the name before. He goes way back with us.'

'CIA trained?'

Vasquez nodded. 'Sherali is an old mujahideen fighter. He stayed out of the civil war with the Taliban, and his warlord wouldn't throw in with us against them after 9/11, either.'

'So how is the CIA involved?'

'Because sometimes it's just as valuable to pay someone to stay out of the fight as it is to pay them to join in. We paid them off to not throw in with the Taliban. As one of the conditions, and in the hopes it would fully bring them over, the company also gave training to the warlord's men. Nothing cutting edge, just basic infantry stuff that you'd learn in the first few weeks of bootcamp.'

'There must have been a lot of people involved. How did you remember Sherali?'

'You know how in every job, every business, there are some people who just jump out? They're different. Better. That was Sherali. Once our guys found out he'd fought against the Russians they pressed him for stories, and those got relayed. Even accounting for Chinese whispers, and stories being embellished as they pass from person to person, the guy had done some shit. And now, it looks like he's doing some more. That's bad.'

'How can you be sure it's the same Sherali?'

'The clue was the discipline of his men. Like I said, nothing high speed, but enough basic field discipline to hint at some Western training. And then there was the video. I sent it to a field office back in the States and got two of the old team to come in and review it. They'd met Sherali first hand. Both Dari speakers. They confirmed that our guys were on the button, that the voice in the kidnap video not only sounded like Sherali, but it matched his tone and cadence and pattern of speech. We're 99 per cent sure that this is our guy.'

'And that's bad?'

'It's worse than if he was just some goat fucker who'd picked up a rifle to try and make a buck. If half the stories are true, he's killed more Russians than Rambo 3.'

'*Rambo III* was a movie, not a person.'

Vasquez pulled out a pack of Newports and offered one to his smoking partner in crime before lighting one up himself.

'I bet you've never seen a Rambo movie.'

CHAPTER 53

Allen opened his eyes. Dappled light was coming through the camouflage netting above him, and the trees above that. The pieces of sky he could see were pale blue and clear. The air was still and fresh. Sometimes he felt like this country was paradise on earth. Allen had travelled all over the world and he hadn't seen anywhere as beautiful as Afghanistan. Its mountains dwarfed Scotland's, and its sunsets were so vivid in their colours that it felt like he was looking at a Bob Ross painting. Allen wasn't usually one for TV but he loved watching that man work. Not because he loved art, but because he appreciated mastery. Ross was a master of his craft, and Allen aspired to be a master at his.

Banks didn't acknowledge him. He was looking down towards the cave through a small telescope mounted on a hand-sized tripod. The kind of set-up one might use for bird watching.

Allen didn't speak. Instead he picked up the notepad beside the telescope and looked at the log: it was as good as empty. No one had come to or gone from the cave. At 1117 hours there had been a brief glimpse of a man at the cave mouth, and that was it. The man had loitered for three seconds then gone back inside. He had been carrying an AK-47. Banks had written a description of the man, and that he had good trigger discipline. His trigger finger rested over its guard.

Allen asked the SEAL the obvious. 'Who do you think trained them?'

'The company, maybe. Or the ISI.' The ISI were Pakistan's version of the CIA, and had a long history of interfering in Afghanistan's affairs. Believable rumours said that they armed and trained the Taliban in Pakistan before sending them across the border to fight. There was nothing too unusual in that except that Pakistan was supposed to be America's ally. They certainly received a huge amount of aid from them. As though this wasn't enough, in 2011 it became apparent that Osama bin Laden – America's most wanted man – was being sheltered in a town run by the ISI. The US had sent in SEAL Team Six to deal with him, and had trusted the Pakistanis so little that they hadn't even told Pakistan about the raid. With friends like that, Allen wondered, who needed enemies?

'Hard to believe those guys were hiding bin Laden all that time,' he said to Banks.

'Yeah,' the SEAL replied. Something in his tone was hard and final as the American moved back into the hide, lay on his back, and pulled his bush hat down over his face.

Allen was now on stag.

CHAPTER 54

Umid cursed to himself as he scrubbed at the pan that was used to cook his brothers' meals. The bottom of it was black from flames and on the inside pieces of meat had burnt themselves onto the metal. Umid knew that some of the pieces had been there for days, the other men not as fastidious as him in their daily duty, but Umid's father had high standards, and if he was given a task, he would do it well.

'If you rub that any harder it might fall apart,' someone said from behind him.

Umid recognised Sherali's voice. The man's tone was as solid and mighty as the mountain that housed them. Umid couldn't imagine that this man had ever felt fear, or doubt. He sounded so sure. So dependable. In that moment, Umid resolved that he would learn to speak in the same way. He would learn everything he could from the man, even down to his speech.

'Is there more water I could use?' he asked the older man.

'No, we need to ration what we have. We could be here for a long time, Umid.'

'Oh.'

'You miss the sun? I know how that feels. When I was a mujahid I often felt more like a scorpion than a soldier of God. But of course, when we came out from under our rocks, then we made the enemy aware of our sting.'

'I wish I'd been there,' Umid said honestly.

'I often thank God that I was born when I was. I was fortunate to be a part of jihad.'

'Even though your family ...' Umid tailed off, thinking of the ruined village where Sherali's family had died. 'You have sons?' he asked after a moment.

'All dead. One died as a child. Three in a feud.'

'A feud?' Umid asked. 'With whom?'

'What does it matter? They are dead now,' Sherali said, leaving no doubt who had caused their ends.

'How many men have you killed?'

'How many sunsets have you seen? I don't count, Umid. I did, when I was young, but I soon learned that it was only the first that mattered. That is when we unlock something inside of ourselves, and see ourselves for who we are. Some can do it, some cannot. I'm sure Daler has already explained this to you. He's very fond of you, Umid. Stay close to him. You will learn a lot.'

'I will.'

'He told me that you handled yourself well on guard with the women.'

'All I had to do was stand there.'

'Yes, but it is not easy to stand in front of someone that you thought you had killed. You have had many tests today, and you have passed them all. Your father would be proud.'

Umid smiled. 'Do you really think so?'

'Of course. Every father is proud when his son becomes a man. It is sad that you do not have a father any more.'

Umid dared to hope that Sherali was proud of him, too, and that hope was rewarded as Sherali pulled a Choora dagger from his wristband and held it out to him.

'For you. A man should have a knife of his own to pass on to his children.'

Umid slowly drew the thin ancient blade from its leather scabbard. The Choora was designed hundreds of years ago by tribes in the Khyber Pass to penetrate chain mail armour, and had been used against all invaders since.

Umid marvelled at the wear and indentations the blade had collected over the many years it had been worn.

Sherali was very proud. 'This was my father's, who gave it to me when the Russian invaders came. It has killed many, and now it will continue to do so.'

Umid re-sheathed the knife into the scabbard and tucked it into his waistband. He was a man, an equal.

'What happens next?' he asked the old bandit.

'They have until darkness to meet our demands. If they do not, we will look at other options.'

'... killing them?' Umid asked, a sense of relief washing over him as Sherali shook his head.

'No one will pay for bodies, Umid. At least not well. No. If the government will not meet our price, then perhaps someone else will.'

CHAPTER 55

BAGRAM

'We're in trouble.' Vasquez sat with Powell in his office as the 2i/c of NATO stood waiting to know what kind of trouble. He had to deal with many kinds of trouble every day.

'We intercepted a call from Sherali to his boss. He has made it clear that he doesn't trust the Republic's government to come through on the demands, and he has another suggestion: sell the hostages to the Taliban.'

The second in command nodded in agreement. 'It was always a possibility. I'd be thinking about that myself about now. Local Taliban, I presume?'

Vasquez nodded. He knew his subject well. 'Their presence in Badakhshan isn't as strong as it is in many parts of the country, but they have people everywhere. If they want the hostages, they can make it happen.'

'Do they have that kind of money?'

'That and more. They're well funded from supporters in Pakistan and the Middle East, not to mention the money they bring in from the opium crops. Any demand won't be a problem to them.'

The 2i/c grabbed himself a chair. This was going to take longer than he first thought.

'But the Taliban can't get their man free.'

'No, but at this point they may be willing to forgo that.

It's been days since the first demand and they've probably figured out that it's all a stall. We need to take this threat as credible. Very credible, and very high risk.'

The former director of UKSF sat forward. 'The sell? What would that mean for the hostages?'

Vasquez looked at Powell, who answered. 'There are a few possibilities. The first is that the Taliban use the hostages to continue the same kind of play that the kidnappers are making. Maybe money, but definitely an exchange of prisoners. Given the bargaining power that they have with the Brit in particular, we think it's unlikely that they would kill the hostages without trying to bargain with them first. And, unlike these kidnappers, the Taliban will have the stomach for a longer negotiation.'

'And there's something else,' Vasquez said. 'With their power and connections, and Badakhshan's proximity to neighbouring countries, it's not unreasonable to expect that they'd take them across the border. They've got choices. Pakistan or any of the northern Stans or even China – then we would need to violate a sovereign nation's territory to get them back.'

'We've done that before,' the 2i/c said.

'But China? Really?'

No, and no one had to say it.

'All this is based on the idea that they would want to hang on to the hostages to negotiate with *us*. But they could just as well mark them up and sell them on to AQ. Then we watch four heads roll off shoulders and into the dust,' Vasquez said.

The 2i/c checked his watch. 'We have just over eight hours before first light. Fede, how long would it take for the Taliban to make it to the cave, assuming they use their people already in-province?

'A couple of hours.'

'Okay, the teams are 10 minutes max to rotors turning, then 30 minutes in the air to target.'

The 2i/c continued to stare at his watch for another 15 seconds but not to count time.

'Okay. So we have time on our side – but only if we know they are heading to the cave. Fede, I want you to widen the surveillance area of the drones. If you need more, you've got them.'

'I'll get on it.'

'And we'll get some ground support A-10s on station too. We need to deal with anything coming towards the cave before a Deliberate Option goes in.'

Powell was liking this idea and was already working on how to sell it to London. Vasquez was more cautious.

'But if we do hit the Taliban too early the Deliberate Option would be compromised before they took any action, and we are back to square one with what the fuck they would do to the hostages.'

The 2i/c had already thought that during his 15-second deliberation.

'The Taliban haven't been contacted, or even agreed yet, right?'

'Correct. We're listening in on the calls made by Sherali's boss's phone, and so far none have gone out. There's a high possibility he is using one phone exclusively to talk to the kidnap team and another for the Taliban and that one we don't have.'

'And I assume you're trying to change that?'

'We are, yes. Both tech and human. All of our assets are on this.'

'Even so,' Powell spoke up, 'it may be that the first notice we get is when the kidnappers are notified.'

The 2i/c leaned forward and looked around the room. 'We cannot allow the hostages to be passed off to the Taliban. Does anyone disagree?'

'I don't disagree,' Powell said, 'but there may be an opportunity to hit them at the exchange, or en route to it, if it doesn't take place at the cave. That's if we get the intelligence. But it would be a higher chance of success for your people.'

The 2i/c nodded. 'Fair one, but we know where the hostages are static, and we know the numbers we're up against. We go in the cave ASAP.'

Powell didn't have to think long about the 2i/c process. 'Agreed.'

He was already standing up to end the meeting. 'I'll convince my boss.' He pointed to Powell. 'You do the same to London. One way or another, we must not lose control of this thing.'

CHAPTER 56

KABUL

It was just over an hour since Powell had left the CIA 'facility' in Bagram and arrived back in the embassy's secure comms basement. Now, for the first time, she was sitting alone facing the bureaucrat on the screen. The events on the ground had moved on during her Black Hawk flight to Kabul. The Taliban had agreed to buy the hostages.

'I expect this means that things have taken a turn for the worst?' The bureaucrat, too, sat alone in front of a plain white wall, in an open-neck shirt and pullover.

Powell checked the time and date digits at the bottom of the satlink screen. It was a Sunday. Days of the week were details Powell hadn't kept track of since being posted to Afghanistan. They were irrelevant. Time had just rolled into one big cycle of work and grabbing some sleep whenever she could.

'They have indeed. At 21.56 local, the kidnappers received a phone call telling them to expect their buyers to be at the cave by first light. That's tomorrow, Monday, and first light is at 05.38 local.'

Powell left the maths of how long they had until the handover for the bureaucrat.

'The name Shah Roshan, a Taliban commander known to be from Badakhshan, was flagged up on the call.'

'Well that's good news.'

'It is and it isn't. Roshan has been off our radars for a long time. So long in fact that he was presumed dead. We don't know where he's coming from, or how many men he'll have with him. It could be anything from a few bodyguards to hundreds of fighters. He commanded a sizable force in the civil war against the Northern Alliance, mostly Pashtos, who are the Taliban majority, but a minority in the north. We're working on tracking him down now.'

'So we have about six hours until this Roshan or whoever will take the hostages.'

'Correct. And we must assume that Roshan's group will be taking the women until we learn otherwise.'

Powell needed to be as concise as she could. Time talking was time lost on the ground.

'If we do not have the go now for a Deliberate Option, in six hours we will lose control of the hostages. For now, we know the women are still in the cave, we know the layout of the interior and how many are holding them, and with what. But once they are handed over ...'

Powell let the bureaucrat work that one out for himself. He did, but still needed more information; his job was also to sell.

'So why not wait until the Taliban pick up the hostages and rescue them en route to wherever they would be heading? Daylight, open ground, wouldn't that be safer?'

'No, because we do not know the routes, we do not know the numbers in the group, and so the success of a rescue attempt would be low. Unfortunately, the Taliban has a say, too, and the women would be dead within the first minute of the attack.'

Powell tried to make her statements more intimate to get the answer she wanted: they were women, not just hostages.

The bureaucrat, however, had got the answer he was looking for. It narrowed down the options for his boss, and so he could make a quicker decision.

But Powell still hadn't got the answer she wanted.

'I agreed with our first position of negotiation, but with events on the ground unfolding as they are, it is clear that a Deliberate Option is the only way there is any chance of these women being rescued.'

The bureaucrat agreed with a nod that could have been saying yes to milk being added to his coffee.

'The prime minister is in Oxfordshire having dinner with the Qatari royal family.'

'I think he needs to be pulled away from his profiteroles and be told we need the go – right now.'

'Correct.'

The bureaucrat stood, before crouching down to keep his face in focus, even if it was too close. 'Wait there, please.'

The bureaucrat walked away leaving just a white-walled screen.

Powell focused on the screen's timer as the most important phone call of her life was happening, and yet she had no control over what decision would come out of it. She went into her pocket to light up a Newport, and then remembered that she had entered the room sterile. All her personal belongings were in a tray and held by the security team and she only got them back on leaving the embassy. All she could do was wait.

Exactly 19 minutes passed before the bureaucrat returned, settled back into his chair, and quickly gathered his thoughts before leaning forward into the lens.

'You have a go. And thank you, *Miss* Powell.'

CHAPTER 57

FOB FAYZABAD, BADAKHSHAN

The teams had stayed stood-to in case ER was needed to extract the OP team if they were compromised or a fastball go was given.

All the while, they carried on preparing with one eye always on the intelligence boards in the ops room. These were constantly updated with satellite imagery of the area, besides Baz's drawing of the cave interior, pictures of the hostages, their formal names, and that they had no nicknames they would react to under stress, details of the mobile phone conversations and, finally and most importantly, the breakdown of the teams now they'd been given the go.

Though the operators were excited to know they were about to be let off the chain, there was no air of jubilation. This was just the beginning.

Coates took control. 'Okay, listen in. This operation is of the utmost importance, not just for the lives of the hostages but for the future of special forces work. When we pull this off, we not only prove to the world that you don't fuck with us and get away with it, we prove to our masters that it should always be us who get the job. No negotiation, no reluctance to deploy us. This is to go more like bin Laden than Qala-i-Jangi. Get in – get out. Job done.'

The battle of Qala-i-Jangi fortress had taken place in 2001 when Taliban prisoners had overwhelmed their captors. It had taken six days of fighting and dozens of air strikes to finally quell the uprising.

Miller liked what he was hearing. This was why he'd joined the navy the day after 9/11: to carry American justice to those who would fuck with his people and their allies. Coates continued with the meet.

'Orders for the Deliberate Option: Ground. Badakhshan Province. You know the HLS. You know the target.' The teams had the satellite imagery, and knew the valley where they'd be dropped off. They also knew the route the OP had taken over the mountain ridge and into the next valley – and the target.

'Situation: The OP team had eyes on all four hostages just before first light this morning. They were in good order and able to move without any aid. Since then, they haven't been seen but have not left the cave. It is assumed they are still alive, as there has been no gunfire or anything else to make us assume otherwise.

'That's the situation now; however that changes at or by first light. Intelligence suggests that a Taliban leader named Shah Roshan will then be on target to take the hostages – where to, we just don't know. The only upside is that the hostages should still be breathing – why would Roshan want dead ones? He'll want to make that happen himself. Questions?'

An American voice shouted from the back. 'How many guys is he rolling with?'

'I'm coming to that now. I know the orders format is different to what you are used to, but stay with me.

'Enemy forces: Inside the cave the OP has seen 12 fighting-age males armed with AKs and some also have sidearms. The bandits' leader is mujahideen who fought against the Soviets and clearly knows what he is doing. They are disciplined, weapons are in good order, and it must be assumed they will fight. Roshan could arrive with anything from a handful to hundreds. His group are well armed and experienced, and they will fight – so we need this done before they turn up.

'Friendly Forces: The ground teams and air assets of surveillance and ground support you are already aware of.

'Mission: To rescue the hostages. Mission: To rescue the hostages.'

Coates paused so that the mission statement could be embedded into everyone's skull. The mission is always repeated, to avoid any confusion about why they are on the ground. Everything the teams do must be about achieving the mission statement.

'Okay, Execution: This will be in three phases. Infiltration, actions on target, exfiltration.

'Infiltration: The four Black Hawk call signs will set us down in the same valley the OP team infiltrated. We'll have an Apache two-ship as top cover. Flight time approximately 45 minutes, with a decoy. From the valley we move on foot to target, where we will RV with the OP team. It took them approximately three hours carrying their OP kit and rigs. We will be well inside their time.'

The teams would be carrying the minimum required: body plates, ammunition, water, trauma care, comms.

Coates continued.

'Actions on target. The two problems we have are the cave and arrival of Roshan. So, you are broken down into three groups. Assault group, cut-off east and cut-off west.'

It was highly likely that Roshan and his group would arrive by vehicle, and therefore would have to come from either end of the valley that ran east to west. One cut-off was an SAS call sign, the other belonged to the SEALs.

The assault team would consist of both Brits and Americans, but it would be the Brit team that was first into the cave. This was politics at play: Brit hostage, Brit assault team up front.

'The OP team will lead the assault team to their start line and return to their OP position, where I will set up the option command point. Once the cut-offs are in position, and on my command, the assault team will make entry into the cave and extract the hostages.

'Cut-offs: you will stop anything entering the valley or anyone from that cave exiting it.'

Coates liked giving orders to SF as they were so concise. Everyone knew what they needed to do, how they were going to do it, and what they needed to take with them to make it happen. Anyone telling them otherwise would be told to wind their necks in. These teams knew their job: speed, surprise and violence of action. The cut-offs would position themselves to be able to do their job, and the assault teams knew how to get into the cave, and coordinate the fight inside a confined space whilst getting the hostages out.

'Action on exfil: The Black Hawk call signs will enter the target valley one at a time, on blue, in the clearing close to the target cave, or if the cut-offs identify an LS near them, they will bring them in on blue instead of moving back to the target cave. That will be sorted out on the ground.

'Order of lift: UK assault team with hostages, US assault team, east cut-off, then west with option command.'

'On blue' meant the colour of smoke that would be used to bring the aircraft in. It had nothing to do with concealment and protection, however; that was what the Apache two-ship was for. It was so that as the pilots flew their aircraft into the valley, they had information on where exactly the ground call signs needed them to land, and more information about wind direction and strength.

'Questions?'

One of the Brit assaulters had something on his mind. 'Suicide vests?'

'The bandits are in it for the money, and the assessment is that they are in no rush to go to paradise, but Roshan's group ... they are coming for just a pick-up – but as always, we will assume they will be worn.'

Coates always used progressive and positive words when giving orders and on the ground. There was never any doubt, never any maybe, should be or hopefully. Rather: We will. We will be. We will have. Operations were a physical event; it was about dealing with situations, not thinking about them.

There were no more questions.

'Okay, on the pad in five.'

CHAPTER 58

Allen listened to the last of the sat phone messages that outlined the plan of what was to come.

'Roger that,' he said into the handset. 'Out.'

In the darkness he felt Banks's eyes on him. Allen passed on the details of the mission.

Finally Banks said what they were both thinking. 'Just to the start line? I don't like our part in it.'

Neither did Allen.

Allen tried to console himself with the thought that there would be other jobs, but he couldn't quite bring himself to believe it. Hostage rescues were rare, and a soldier's chance to be a part of one were few and far between. One SAS squadron had counter-terrorism duties at a time, which made the chances of landing a gig like this rare. Even when they did come up, only a few men took part. There were more than 100 SAS operators in Afghanistan tonight but only 24 of them were taking part in this mission. A special forces soldier needed luck too, and Allen believed his had run out in the Korengal Valley. That was how it went for so many high performers. Allen felt like the boxing champion who couldn't get one more shot at reclaiming his title. The CEO who gets voted off by his own board members. Very few people got to choose when to end their dream. People like Allen did not know the word 'quit'. They wouldn't have been able to do the things that got them to where they were if they were wired any other way.

Without thinking, Allen found himself uttering the one line from a film that had always stuck with him.

'A guy told me one time, don't let yourself get attached to anything that you aren't willing to walk out on in 30 seconds flat when you feel the heat coming around the corner.'

'Great movie,' Banks said. 'It's not realistic, though.'

'The film?'

'No, they did it right. I mean the line. What kind of life is it if you never find something that's worth facing the heat for? I joined the teams because I want to feel that. I want something that I'm terrified of losing.'

Allen had to agree. It wasn't a conversation that he had expected to have with Banks, but knowing that the coming dawn would bring bloodshed had a way of loosening men's lips. It wasn't that Allen worried for himself, but by first light some of his friends might no longer be walking the earth. He imagined Banks felt the same way.

'This part is shit, isn't it?' Allen said. 'The waiting game.'

'Yeah,' Banks replied in a hushed tone. For a moment it sounded like that was all that he would say, then the SEAL went on with a quiet intensity. 'I feel just like I did when the bin Laden raid went in. Pissed off, and nervous.'

'Everyone came out of that alive,' Allen said.

'Yeah,' Banks replied quietly. 'Yeah.'

The two men lapsed into silence, thinking of old friends passed, and praying that more names would not be added to that list.

The valley was still and silent. Allen knew it wouldn't last. In the morning gunfire would echo through the mountains and men would breathe their last breaths. That was the life he had chosen. He was a volunteer; no one had made him become a soldier. If he didn't like it, he could get out. But he hadn't, because this was what he did. He couldn't walk away from soldiering any more than a mother could from her child.

CHAPTER 59

BAGRAM

Rachael Powell stared up at the Afghan night sky. Even with the light pollution of the base, it was stunning, an infinite carpet of lights pin-pricking through the deep purples and black. It was one of the things she would miss about this country when her time here came to an end. What she wouldn't miss was the feeling of guilt she always had when others were going in to risk their lives on a mission that she had helped to shape.

Powell heard someone approaching the smoking area – a few plastic chairs surrounded by dirt-filled HESCO bastions – and smiled when she saw it was Federico Vasquez. She'd worked with a lot of Americans in her career, as Britain and the US were intertwined in almost all of their conflicts. She'd found some to be brash and arrogant, their egos inflated by the might of America's military. Others, like Vasquez, truly wanted the world to be a better place, and believed in the ideals of personal liberty and freedom. Powell handed her packet of Newports over to him as he took a seat in the plastic chair beside her.

'Appreciate it,' he said, striking up the smoke. Vasquez sensed that he'd walked into a moment of reflection and took a few thoughtful drags on his cigarette before speaking, his eyes following Powell's up to the stars. 'I reckon a lot of people have come to this country and looked up at those stars before a fight. Your British Empire soldiers, a couple of times. Russians. Macedonians and Greeks under Alexander.

'What this country needs is to become the Switzerland of Central Asia. No one fucks with the Swiss. Even that crazy fuck Hitler knew better. People think that he laid off them because he didn't want to fuck with that wealth, but come on, that's exactly what he would have wanted to take for himself. He didn't do it because it would have been too costly. The mountains, the people, it would have been a bloodbath. Instead people just play ball. But for some reason, in this place … I don't know if I believe in curses, but it's hard not to when you see what the people in this country have gone through.'

'That's not a curse, Fede. It's just human nature.'

'Same thing, right?' he took another drag on his cigarette. 'Shit, the stars really pull out the philosophy, huh?'

When Vasquez struck up a second cigarette, Powell knew that his flippant comments were just a mask.

'So what do you think their chances are?' she asked him.

'Of getting all four out alive?' He blew out a long cloud of smoke. 'Not good. You?'

'Not good.'

'I don't put anything past those guys, but some things just aren't built for success. If they were in a compound, and we could hit from multiple directions, I'd feel better about it, but with the hostages tucked away at the back of a cave and only one way in? I don't like it.'

'Would you call it off? If you could?'

Vasquez shook his head. 'Not my call.'

'But if it was?'

'Then I'd say it's not my call. This is one for the teams. They know the stakes. If they want to go in, then I say go in. It's not my ass hanging in the breeze.'

'Yeah,' Powell agreed, feeling the guilt again. 'That's the only thing I hate about this job. If it goes well it's good for all of us. How we feel about ourselves and our careers, but if it goes bad …'

'It might hurt our job prospects, but we're still alive.'

'Right.'

'I feel you, but everyone involved in this made a choice.'

'I suppose that's true. I just wish I could go in with them. Share some of the risk.'

'Well you go ahead.' He smiled. 'I tried that shit once. Not for me.'

'You did?'

'First thing the company did with a name like mine was ship my Latino ass south of the border.'

'Doing what?'

'Things that made me glad to be behind a desk for the rest of my career. And honestly, things that made me appreciate what we're doing here. We might not always do it the right way, but we do have the chance to change this country for the better. That means something.'

Powell nodded. 'I feel the same way. I think we can leave this place better than we found it.'

'We can.' Vasquez nodded. 'But we're going to have to crush some skulls along the way.'

Powell was okay with that. She sat back in her chair and looked back up at the stars.

CHAPTER 60

Umid stood a couple of metres back from the cave's entrance and gazed up at the same stars as Powell. The past day had felt like a lifetime, and he had aged with it. For the first time in his life he had been prepared to take a life, and then he had to face the woman that he was willing to kill. It had left him exhausted. He wondered if it would get easier with time. He didn't feel bad about his actions but he wasn't proud either. When he thought back on the moment when he pulled the trigger it was like he was watching himself from above, and someone else had been the one holding the gun. He didn't expect that Tasneem would forgive him and he didn't know if he cared. He just knew that he would be glad when the Taliban came in the morning and took the women away. The excitement he had felt when they first captured them had turned to weariness. It had been an adventure, but it was an adventure that he was ready to be over.

The prospect of money and what it would bring him was a salve on his thoughts. He had been willing to take a life – and would do so again – so that he could bring his own children into the world. Without money he could have no wife. Without a wife he could have no children. It was as simple as that. And so, Umid knew that he would have to do things that he would rather not have to do. So be it. That was reality. That was life. No one had ever said that being a man would be easy.

The sound of Daler pissing against the cave wall snapped him from his thoughts.

'Can't you do that outside?' Umid asked him. 'It's starting to stink in here.'

'You know Sherali's orders,' Daler replied. 'No one is to go outside.'

That gave Umid pause for thought. 'Do you really think they could be watching us?'

'How would they know where to look? But you know what the Americans are like. They always have planes in the sky looking to kill Afghans. If they see us walking here they will drop bombs on us, just because they can and they hate us.'

'I've never met an American,' Umid said. 'Have you?'

'No, but if I did I would kill them. I don't like the Taliban either but at least they are Afghans.'

'Do you know their commander that's coming for the hostages?'

'Roshan? Only by reputation. Sherali says he is a good fighter.'

'If Sherali says that then it must be true,' Umid said.

'Why are you so sad, Umid? You should be happy. Tomorrow we'll be wealthy men.'

'Yes.'

'You've been thinking about that woman? Don't. She's as bad as the Americans. Worse, even. I've heard these people cut the hearts from babies. They eat them.'

'The Americans?'

'Of course the Americans.'

'How do you know this?'

'Everyone knows this.'

'My father didn't ever speak of this.'

'Maybe he was trying to protect you from the reality of the world,' Daler allowed. 'But a man can't hide from evil, Umid. He has to face it, and fight it. Like you did.'

He patted Umid on the shoulder. It was a small gesture, but it meant the world to the young man.

Umid heard the blankets being pulled back behind them. For a second in the light he saw Sherali, and then the bandit leader stood beside him.

'Daler. Umid. I have a job for you.'

CHAPTER 61

CREECH AIR FORCE BASE, NEVADA, USA

Sarah Cohen leaned back in her flight seat and stretched her arms towards the ceiling. Piloting a drone meant long hours sitting still, and at the end of each mission she always felt like she'd shrunk a couple of inches in height as her spine compressed and her muscles tightened. There was a physical aspect to piloting aircraft, but a different kind of physicality was needed for drone work. She often compared it to the difference between an infantry soldier and a sniper. Piloting a Predator meant hours of stillness, watching and waiting. Occasionally a shot would follow, but a drone operator required patience above aggression.

Cohen was pleased that her unit commander had given her and her crew the flight that would oversee the endgame of the hostage rescue. Things often didn't work out like that, and a mission would be handed off like a relay baton from one team to the next. Cohen suspected that she knew the motivation behind her commander's decision: three weeks ago, Cohen's crew had been tasked with taking out a high value target that was in transit between safe houses. The Predator's Hellfire Missile had scored a clean hit on the vehicle, taking out an enemy of America and the Afghan Republic, but it had come at a cost. Inside the vehicle were the target's two young children. They had died for the sins of their father. After the mission debrief Cohen had gone to her suburban home in Henderson where her own two children were fast asleep. She knew that there was a price to pay for freedom, but that didn't mean that paying it came without a cost to her conscience. She was sure that her commander had given her this hostage rescue flight so that she could be a part of a mission that was to save innocent lives, and not to take them.

In her career, Cohen had provided overhead surveillance for hundreds of special operations raids. It was a thrill to see the thermal images of America's best hunting down their enemies like a wolf pack. Cohen could proudly say that she and her crew had helped save American lives by spotting enemy fighters waiting in ambush and the 'squirters' who tried to sneak away to fight another day. From American soil, Cohen's crew helped take the war to her nation's enemies in far-flung corners of the world. Tonight, they would help rescue four innocent people and bring justice to those who had taken them. It was a thought that put a smile on the pilot's face, but it wasn't a smile that lasted more than a few seconds.

'Shit,' her analyst said beside her.

Several thermal shapes had appeared from the cave mouth. Five were armed. Two were not.

'Fuck.' Cohen's voice was grim. 'They're splitting up the hostages.'

CHAPTER 62

Umid had wanted to leave the cave and feel the air on his face, but the moment had not brought the joy that he had expected. Sherali had ordered Daler to take Umid, three other men and two of the hostages to a second cave.

'Wait there until I come for you,' the bandit leader had explained. 'Roshan is not kin, I don't trust him. If I was him I'd bottle us up in the cave and make us hand over the hostages for our own lives, and not the money, so we'll split up. If he attacks us we'll squeeze him between us.'

'You think it will come to that?' Daler had asked.

'No.' The old mujahid shook his head. 'But I've lived this long by expecting the unexpected.'

'As you say, Sherali. But shouldn't we keep the hostages together?'

Sherali shook his head. 'The Taliban aren't interested in the two Afghan women. They will kill them out of hand.'

'So what?' Daler had asked, matter of fact. 'If they buy them they can do as they wish.'

'They won't buy them, that's the point. They're only interested in the British one, and the African. We can still ransom the others, or sell them off to someone.'

'They're too old to be brides,' Daler had replied.

'The younger one is pretty,' Sherali told him. 'The

other can clean, or work a field. Do you want to throw money away?'

'No.'

'Then keep them away from the Taliban. And if the Taliban play us false, do as you must.'

'I will, Sherali.'

Umid couldn't see Tasneem's face in the darkness but he could feel her stare burning into him. Was she a witch, as Daler had claimed?

One of the men stumbled and cursed in the darkness. There was a moon in the sky but the tall mountains cast long shadows across the valley.

'It's up here,' one of the bandits said. He was an older man and knew the valleys and peaks like the back of his rough, calloused hand.

They entered the new cave through a narrow entrance that was little wider than a man. Unlike the cave they had left this one had only one large chamber. One of the men used a torch to illuminate the inside. As Daler pushed the two captives into a corner, Umid and the others set their provisions down. They had not carried much. Sherali had arranged for them to be collected by pickup truck the next day. There was no point in staying in the caves once the hostages had been sold to the Taliban. Sherali said that they would be able to sell the two Afghan women quickly, and then the men would be free to collect their wages from the boss.

'Umid,' Daler said. 'It's still your watch. You keep your eyes on the women. I'll put a man on the entrance and the rest of us will sleep. Wake me up before dawn.'

Umid didn't remind Daler that he had also been on watch. With command – even a small one – came privileges.

'Yes, Daler.'

'And remember who they are,' he said, looking at the hostages.

'Yes, Daler.'

Tasneem had the sense to wait for the men to fall asleep before she spoke. 'Umid,' she said quietly. 'Help us. I know you're a good man, Umid. Help us, please. Help us escape.'

Umid felt his hand move before he had a chance to think about it. The back of it struck Tasneem hard across the face.

'Be silent,' he told her. 'Or I will do it again.'

Umid was a boy no longer. Tomorrow he would be a wealthy man.

CHAPTER 63

FOB FAYZABAD, BADAKHSHAN

When the war was over, and Miller left the service, there were a few things that he knew he would miss forever. His brothers, of course, though he could form strong bonds with the men he worked a ranch with. Even pulling on his gear and shouldering his rifle was something that he could feel out on the frontiers of home. But the sound of helicopter engines whining to life, their rotors spinning up, and hot rotor wash and the smell of avgas passing over him as he prepared to go into the fight? No. There was no substitute in life for that, and no matter how many times Miller had experienced it, it would never be enough.

'Ready to work?' Taff shouted at him as they waited on the helicopter pad to board, the SAS trooper's face brown and green with camouflage cream.

'Yessir.'

'It'll be good to see Allen,' Taff said. 'But he's going to be pissed off that he's not on the assault.'

'He'll get over it,' Miller said, not believing a word of it. Both he and Taff were part of the teams that would be hitting the cave. Miller knew that by the time the sun came up he might be treating the Brit and his teammates as casualties. Or worse, carrying their bodies out of the cave. That was part of the job, but it didn't mean that it didn't enter his mind. Miller knew some guys who could just block it out, but not him. He wasn't scared of death, or of thinking about it. He'd learned about it from a young age, and it was what it was. God had a plan for everyone, and if God's plan was that Miller died in the service of his country, then he was okay with that. What better way to leave this world than protecting the nation that he loved so dearly? Miller might have been one of those people who wrapped himself in his flag, but he was also one of the few who had earned the right to do so.

The Black Hawks' rotors had picked up to full speed. Miller was about to put out his hand to the Brit when he saw Coates running towards them.

'Everyone on me!' the officer shouted. Quickly, a huddle formed around him. Coates shouted against the rotor wash to be heard. 'The hostages have been split up. Two are still in the target cave, the other two have been moved to another cave, close by.'

Coates gave it a second or two, making sure he had been understood.

'This is what will now happen. The cut-offs will stay as they are, the assault team will split in two. The target cave is now cave Alpha and will be taken by the Brits. The new cave is now cave Bravo and will be taken by the US. The OP team will take both teams to their start lines. Questions?'

'How many longs in the second cave?' a SEAL asked. He wanted to know how many AKs – and the men to use them.

'Five. No more questions, no time. Mount up.'

CHAPTER 64

Steve Ream looked out from his cockpit and felt a surge of adrenaline as he saw the line of special forces operators making their way to his aircraft. They wore a variety of chest rigs, webbing and patrol sacks, helmets and goggles on their heads, skin smeared with camouflage cream, weapons slung across their bodies or cradled in one hand.

It didn't matter how many times he saw this scene heading towards his aircraft it always made Ream think about his uncle, who had been a marine in Vietnam. Uncle Joey wasn't one of those guys who 'didn't wanna talk about it' and his stories of fighting in Hue City during the Tet Offensive had been the highlight of Ream's Thanksgivings as a kid. Of course, Uncle Joey had left out most of it. He hadn't talked about the friends he lost, or why he was drinking more than everyone else at the dinner table. Ream had to figure that out for himself, when he lost his first friends in the service. But just like Uncle Joey, he could live with those moments of darkness, because for all of the tough parts of service, this was where he wanted to be: in the thick of the action, surrounded by people who would give it all – even their lives – to see that a job was done, no matter what. Nothing on earth could compare to this feeling.

The operators loaded into the back of his Black Hawk. On some flights men would be laughing and joking and goofing around. Tonight was not one of those nights. The British soldiers he was carrying were as silent as the grave, an intensity in their eyes that Ream had rarely seen, even among elite warriors. He almost pitied the kidnappers that were going to have to face these men, but not quite. They'd chosen their path, and that path would end tonight. The pilot had no doubt that the SAS assault team would be successful. No doubt at all. The only question was at what cost. Ream knew that he would be bringing all of the men back – no man left behind – but how much blood would he and his crew be washing out of the back of the Black Hawk?

The pilot remembered the first time that he'd flown back a man down. They'd been under fire at the landing site and one of the cockpit's windows was frosted. The rounds were stopped by the armoured pilots' seats. He'd had no time to look at what was happening in the back of his aircraft, not when he was trying to navigate telephone lines and tracer fire. But he remembered the stench of blood hitting his nostrils, and he remembered how quiet the sky had sounded when they cleared the LS. Even the beat of the rotors seemed to fade away.

'Good in the back?' Ream asked his crew chief over the crew net. It wasn't a necessary question; his crew chief was all over his job like an ant on jelly, currently counting the soldiers on board.

Ream realised he was feeling nervous. Not the bad kind, the exciting kind, like waiting to return a kick-off in high-school football. That feeling in the pit of your stomach when you're waiting for the referee to blow the whistle before you run downfield and hit someone. It was a good feeling. The kind that let you know that you're alive. Really alive.

Ream got on to the squadron net. 'Reaper One Four complete and ready for take-off.'

The other Black Hawks were loading up, and once ready would be making the same call. Ahead of Ream's aircraft the Apache two-ship lifted into the darkness. Izaak Brown Jnr, the two-ship commander, looked through the lens in his helmet-mounted display that gave him a clear view of the ground from the aircraft's night-vision sensors, part of the sensor suite mounted on the nose of the aircraft.

Amelia Ojeda, his co-pilot, sat in front and slightly below Izaak in the tandem cockpit. Both crew members were capable of flying the aircraft and using the weapon system independently, but Amelia wasn't flying tonight, she was the gunner. Scanning the area through her helmet-mounted display she slaved the 30mm chain gun. Wherever she looked now, the chain gun under the aircraft's forward fuselage followed. If any tracer or RPGs headed at them as they cleared the FOB, Amelia would look and instantly fire her high-explosive rounds into a metre square if needed. If she wanted a larger area attack, she could always use the Hydra 70mm rockets from their 19 missile tube launchers, one on each side of the aircraft, which contained a mixture of high explosive and white phosphorus warheads.

Izaak was busy talking to his other ship on the net and listening to the Black Hawks but now had time to talk to his co-pilot.

'Shit, Mel.'

'What?'

'I forgot my Life Savers.'

Mel laughed, still sweeping the area through the helmet display.

'Disappointing.'

Mel also liked them, and now the night was going to be mint free.

Izaak had been a disappointment to his parents, too, when he joined the military. His father was a Manhattan veterinary surgeon whose average bill of $15,000 to replace overfed and pampered cats' ruined kidneys meant life was good for the Browns. Izaak was privately educated and had all the privileges that money buys as a Harvard student, following in his father's footsteps with plans to take over the family practice.

On 9/11, the 20-year-old student was at home in the family's Upper East Side brownstone and Izaak's life changed in an instant. He saw the Twin Towers collapse just a few miles south; he felt the dust fill his nostrils. It stayed in the air for days afterwards, and so did the nagging feeling that he needed to act. He cut college and joined the military, to his family's dismay. But that was then, and now Major Brown Jnr's parents were very proud.

The Black Hawk flight leader got on the net. He was the most experienced pilot of the four crews, a Boston Ivy League graduate with a laid-back, almost horizontal accent.

'All Reapers are ready for take-off.'

Most pilots sounded uninterested in what they were saying. It was procedural so the job would be done correctly. Izaak was just the same.

'Roger that. All Reaper call signs, you are clear.'

The flight leader came back. 'On my mark. Three, two, one, take-off.'

Ream raised the collective in one hand and guided the Black Hawk into the air with his other hand on the stick. He felt the weight of his human cargo in the controls, and adjusted accordingly. As the helicopter lifted into the sky, the FOB's buildings became smaller and smaller, and in the distance, green through his night vision, the massive mountains of Badakhshan loomed into view.

Ream looked through his cockpit door window and saw the other three Black Hawks rising beside him. Somewhere, high above him in the darkness, the Apaches had eyes on the rising troop-carrying craft like protective sheepdogs. Take-off was a dangerous time for a helicopter, the hovering aircraft a tempting target for an enemy. The flight leader wasted no time in clearing the HLS. Ream followed, dipping the aircraft's nose, and headed south towards Kabul for fifteen minutes as a decoy.

Mel kept monitoring the sensor suite as they shadowed the Black Hawks. This was her second aircrew tour but her first with a SOAR assault company, where life was giving her so much more. Not for nothing was the unit's motto 'Don't Quit'.

The Upper East Side of Manhattan might as well have been on the moon for someone brought up in a low-rent subdivision of Albuquerque, New Mexico. She wasn't an only child but the eldest of four girls. Her mother cleaned a motel's rooms and her father cut its grass. She stayed in the public school system and finished high school, but college was never going to happen for her. That cost the sort of money that mopping and mowing didn't provide.

Amelia wanted more – of what she didn't know, but what she did know was that the route to more for someone like her was through education, and for that she joined the military. Private Ojeda was an eager and brilliant student, and was even able to send a little money home to help the family. But still she wanted more, and so applied to become a pilot. Now, eight years later, Captain Ojeda was flying the world's most powerful and sophisticated flying tank. It wasn't just her family that were so proud of her, it was the whole Albuquerque subdivision.

She felt the aircraft bank to its left and continued to shadow the Black Hawks. They were now clear of any habitation and earshot so had turned east and were pushing towards the mountains.

Mel knew this was the beginning of a very long night with no Life Savers.

CHAPTER 65

Tasneem sat in the darkness and wondered how many hours she had left to live.

She had made peace with death a long time ago. As an Afghan, and as a woman, her life had been violent. She had been 10 years old when the Russians had come, but there had always been danger before them. Bandits and dangerous thieves. Clans at war. Tribal disputes and family feuds. And then there was sickness, in both adults and children. Life expectancy was almost half that of the Western world. Now in her forties, Tasneem was considered an old woman. As a child she had never expected to make this age. Not with the Russians, the civil war that followed and then the Taliban. When that regime had fallen she had dared to hope, but thousands of years of tradition and bloodshed could not be changed in a decade. The men who had taken her and her friends were proof of that.

Tasneem couldn't bring herself to hate the kidnappers any more than she could hate pneumonia or the other sicknesses that stole life in Afghanistan. These bandits were as much a part of her country as the mountains, and she hoped God would forgive them. Not because of what they would do to her, but what they would do to her friends, and what they were doing to the dozens – hundreds, even – of children who would now die because they had not received the care that their aid work could bring.

Did they even understand what they were doing? What the ramifications of their actions were? Laura was British, and the British, for all their faults, came after their own people when they were in danger. Tasneem wondered if even now they were being watched. They had all heard the stories about NATO's special forces and their raids. Even the warriors of Afghanistan feared them. They came unexpectedly in the night, often killing silently and leaving only bodies and terror in their wake. This was why Tasneem expected to die. The British would come for Laura, and when they did, Tasneem and her friends would be killed. Not even the British special forces could rescue hostages from inside of caves guarded by armed men. They would try, and they would fail, Tasneem was sure of that. The question was, when would they come? How many nights did she have left to live?

She had considered telling Umid about what would happen to the bandits, and the British reaction to kidnappers, but in the end Tasneem had decided that it was far more likely to cause the bandits to kill them out of hand and flee than hand the women back safely. They didn't understand that the British desire for vengeance was just as strong as it was in Afghanistan. The Americans, too. For an attack on their country, they had spent 10 years at war across the world, with no end in sight. And so it would be for the kidnappers. They had sealed their fate as soon as they took a Western hostage, Tasneem was sure of that. No matter what happened they would be tracked down and killed.

What surprised her was that Sherali seemed ignorant of this. He was older than her. That he had lived this long meant that he must be either cunning or cowardly, and he did not seem like the frightened type. His men respected him, that was clear. But how had he overlooked what the British reaction would be?

Tasneem had given this question a lot of thought since they had been captured. After all, there wasn't much to occupy her time as a captive in the cave. In the end she had decided that Laura had been targeted precisely because she *was* Western. That was what made her a valuable bargaining chip. Bargaining for what, Tasneem had no idea. Money was her best guess. But it didn't matter. Laura had told her glumly that 'Britain does not negotiate.' Tasneem said this was not true. After all, Britain had negotiated with her own country several times in the wars when the greatest empire on earth had been humbled by Afghan warriors, but Laura had shaken her head and said, 'That was then. This is now. They won't negotiate. They always say so on the TV. The politicians. They always say it.'

And if they would not negotiate, then that meant that they would fight. Expectation of that moment tied Tasneem's nerves into knots. At every moment she expected gunfire to erupt and explosions in the valley. She would have to face death, again.

She thought back to the moment when Umid had pointed the pistol at her face. The weapon was no bigger than a man's hand but it had appeared to her as large as a cannon. She had been aware of every detail – the flecked paint on the barrel, Umid's broken and dirt-ingrained fingernail holding the trigger – and the whole moment had felt like it had unfolded over years. Time had stood still. Her clarity had a focus like she had never known. When she saw the young man squeeze the trigger, she had prepared to meet God, but instead there was only a click that sounded as loud as a bomb going off, and then time moved quickly again, and Tasneem felt sick to her stomach, but too frozen to do anything else but stare at the man who would have killed her.

And yet she didn't hate him. She had not been lying when she said that she recognised her son in Umid. Her boy could have become a bandit if he had been placed on a different path. She did not think Umid was evil. Just that he had been given bad options, and chosen the worst of them.

For that, she was certain he would pay with his life.

CHAPTER 66

FAYZABAD, BADAKHSHAN

Wazir had never considered himself a brave man, just a loyal one. Loyal to God, loyal to his family, loyal to his tribe, and since its creation, loyal to the Republic of Afghanistan and the country's future. That was why he drove his beat-up Corolla taxi about the town, watching and listening to what his rides were doing and talking about.

Born in Badakhshan, Wazir had been 15 years old when the Americans had come to his province. Wazir's father had been delighted. He hated the Taliban with a fierce fury – two of Wazir's uncles had died fighting for the Northern Alliance, and Wazir's father had been wounded in the leg, giving him a limp for the rest of his life. Despite his young age, his father was enthusiastic when Wazir suggested that he offer his services to the Americans. He had thought that maybe he would become a soldier, or that they would train him in some skill that would be needed in the new Republic. A teacher, maybe. Or a bureaucrat.

Instead, they had asked him to be a spy, and so he became one of the CIA's 'human assets'.

Of course, they had never asked him in so many words. Instead, through their interpreters, the Americans had suggested that if he could bring them useful information then he could be rewarded. And then, when he was old enough, they would give him a place in Afghanistan's new military.

And so Wazir had used his young age to move freely around his home town, watching and listening. He soon realised that men were a lot more careless about what they said around boys than around other men, and Wazir would relay what he heard to his handler. He took the money home to his father and was surprised when he saw the horror on his face.

'Do you know what they will do to you if they catch you?'

'It's no different to the risks in battle,' Wazir had replied.

'It's all the difference! You have no chance to fight back, Wazir. You have no brothers who will fight to save you. They will skin you like a goat, but not give you the mercy of slitting your throat first!'

Nothing in Wazir's life, including his own intuition, told him not to continue the work, and so Wazir continued to be a pair of American eyes and ears in Badakhshan. As NATO's grip became tighter on the country, there was less to report, as many of the Taliban hard core died or slipped across the border, and those who had been allies of convenience now switched their allegiance to the victors. His handlers stayed true to their word, and when he reached the recruiting age Wazir was put in for enlistment into the Afghan National Army.

He remembered the moment that he had been rejected like a bad dream. It was seared into his soul. He had a weak heart, they said. 'It was strong enough to spy on the Taliban!' he told them, but they would not give him a uniform.

'You can keep your old job, if you want it,' the American had said, and something in his eyes made Wazir wonder if he truly did have a weak heart, or was an American strong hand the real reason his application had been rejected.

'Get a job,' the American had told him. 'A truck driver would be good. Something that gives you a reason to be on the road and moving between towns. Longer distance would be even better.'

Wazir had done as he was told but decided on a taxi. Trucks got hijacked by bandits, and drivers were killed. Though he had been disappointed not to be able to join the war on the fighting side, at least he was still doing something to aid his country, and with two wages – one from taxi driving and the other clandestine – he was able to start and support a family. Now 25 years old, Wazir had two young daughters whom he loved dearly. He prayed that he would live long enough to have several more children too.

Wazir didn't like his chances of that. Not tonight. His handler had contacted him, and he told him that they had received word that a force of Taliban were mobilising in Badakhshan. 'There's a good reward in it if you find out where, and how many,' the new American had said. He was Wazir's eighth handler. The Americans came and went from the war, but to Wazir the war was insepar- able from his home. If he was caught, it wouldn't only be him that paid the price: the Taliban would slaughter his whole family.

It was for that very reason that Wazir did what he did. Any organisation that was willing to kill innocents deserved to be opposed, and that was why Wazir was driving his taxi around the deserted streets of his home town deep into the night, his eyes on stalks and his heart in his mouth.

As the clock on his Corolla's dash turned to 30 minutes past midnight, he saw them.

CHAPTER 67

Ream took his position as the fourth Black Hawk in a convoy flanked by a pair of Apache gunships. The easy part, the decoy, of the flight was over, high altitude flying over the first of the mountains, but now the fun was about to begin. As the Apache pilots peeled off to provide top cover, the first of the Black Hawks banked hard left as it dropped down towards the deck like the lead car on a roller coaster. One after another the Black Hawks followed, and then it was Ream's turn to head east and out of sight and sound.

'Dropping now,' he said over the internal comms net to alert his crew chief, then Ream pushed his stick forward and adjusted the pitch of the rotors. He felt his stomach rise up as the Black Hawk dropped altitude, the hard green lines of the mountains rushing up to meet him through his night-vision goggles. Ream watched as one, two, three Black Hawks plunged into a valley between the peaks and then it was his turn; the huge expanse of sky vanishing, Ream's Black Hawk suddenly turned into a pinball that needed to bounce from one hard turn to the next without ever touching the sides.

This was what he and the other pilots referred to as 'movie shit'. Those moments where you really had to pinch yourself to believe what you were doing, except there was no time to pinch. No time to do anything else except your job, and only the best in the world could do this, part of a snake of helicopters twisting and turning through the mountains, flying with nothing but a pair of NVGs, a lot of training and a hell of a lot of guts.

Behind Ream, his door gunners had one hand on their miniguns and the other on handles to brace themselves against the sudden turns, which they rode with the ease of a big wave surfer. For the kitted-up troops, the ride was more like being in the back of a violent laundry machine, being tossed from one side to the other with no idea what was coming next, and knowing that at any moment they might hit a mountainside and be wiped out of existence. Their lives were in the hands of the pilot now, and the trust had to be absolute. That was how the military worked. It was a series of exemplary individuals who each had to complete their tasks in order for the larger mission to work. If the pilots botched the insertion, the mission would fail. If the pilots achieved the insertion but the soldiers failed to do their jobs on the ground, the mission would fail. And then there were intelligence assets, air support, command and control, and medical teams on standby. As the recruiting posters said: 'One team. One fight'.

Ream felt himself being pinned back into his seat as he pulled hard into another tight corner. Ahead of him the other Black Hawks were turning and burning, rising and falling as they crested ridges and dropped into the next valley.

The next few minutes became one long moment for Ream, where he was ever present. There was no thought of the future, or of his family, or even of the hostages they were on their way to rescue. There was only one turn, then the next one, and then the next.

And then the flight leader came on to the net: 'Two minutes.'

CHAPTER 68

The two-minute warning had been passed on to the helicopter's pax and they now physically prepped themselves to get their boots on the ground.

Gareth 'Taff' Davies remembered the first time that he'd sat in a helicopter. It had been a Gazelle, a small Army Air Corps model that had come to the town fair and parked in the middle of the rugby field. Like loads of other children, Taff – or 'Sam' as his parents had called him – had stood in line to get the chance to sit in the cockpit. It was one of the most vivid moments of his childhood, and probably one of those that had pointed him in the direction of a career in the forces.

Now being thrown around the back of the Black Hawk like an empty tracksuit, Taff was wondering if he'd made the right decision. The pilot was flying like a pissed-up boy racer. At least that's how it felt in the back. Taff knew that the route they were flying was treacherous and demanded this type of manoeuvring, but that wasn't much consolation when the barrel of someone's rifle caught him square on the jaw. It felt like he'd been kicked by a donkey, but that was all in a day's work. It had been the same when Taff had done long-distance, low-level parachute insertions via C-130s. After spending time being thrown around in the dark, and surrounded by smelly, retching soldiers, you were more than happy to throw yourself into the black void outside the aircraft's door. The same had been true during Taff's first tour, back in Iraq in 2004. It was so hot inside the vehicles that you didn't care what was waiting for you outside. Better to take your chances with an RPG than 42 degrees Celsius in body armour and helmet.

At least kit had come a long way since then. What Taff was wearing now offered more protection but weighed less, and was far less bulky. Taff was glad he'd played rugby himself as a kid. It had got him used to being roughed up on a weekly basis. Being in the Black Hawk was a lot like being in the middle of a ruck, except in pitch darkness. You never knew where the next hit was coming from. You just put your head down and got on with it.

Taff couldn't wait to get off the heli and get on with the job. This was the kind of raid that legends were made of, and he wasn't just a part of it but on the assault team, and with a position at the front of the stack. In the morning he'd either be dead, a failure, or be part of a tiny fraction in an already elite world: special forces soldiers who had rescued a hostage. Out of all of the special operations units, very few men got this chance. The only dampener was that Allen could not be a part of it. He was a grumpy Jock fucker but Taff had learned a lot from him since he'd joined the regiment, and Allen had taken him under his wing. There'd been no song and dance about it, that wasn't Allen's way, but he'd always been there for Taff with advice at the right time, saving him from many a fuck-up. Every soldier needed a mentor, and it was the duty of every senior soldier to mentor the men beneath him. Allen had been that person for Taff and it ate at him that Allen would have to watch the team go in without him.

Suddenly Taff lurched towards the front of the Black Hawk: the helicopter had dropped speed, and as the doors were pulled open avgas fumes and dust engulfed the interior.

CHAPTER 69

Steve Ream's was the first aircraft to be landing; the other three stacked and waited beyond the dust cloud his rotors were now generating.

In a dust landing, it takes the whole crew constantly communicating with each other to reach the ground safely. Every one of the aircrafts' crews tried to keep a visual on the ground with their NVGs through a swirling tornado of dirt.

Taff watched the crew chief, who was lying flat on the deck, his head sticking out of the door, his mouth in constant motion as he replayed to Ream what he could see through the green glow of his night vision. It took less than 30 seconds before Taff felt the bump of the aircraft's wheels making contact with a small area of rock just about capable of taking a Black Hawk.

The crew chief rolled out of the way for his cargo of troops to disgorge from the side doors and run clear of the rotors and dust.

Ream swung his head round and scanned over his shoulder. SAS troopers were piling out of the doors and running off into the night. In seconds they were gone, and his crew chief came on to the net.

'Clear.'

Ream lifted into the sky and dropped the aircraft's nose. The moment he cleared off into the darkness, the second Black Hawk descended into the vortex of dirt and created even more. Ream's crew chief pushed back the doors to keep the thick layer inside the aircraft from swirling about.

Below him, in the valley, the teams were already making distance towards the target.

CHAPTER 70

FAYZABAD, BADAKHSHAN

Wazir watched the group of men milling about their pickup trucks. There were two dozen of them, with four trucks, and though Wazir saw no weapons, he knew that these were the men he had been told to look for. Their mannerisms gave them away. There was an energy about them that should not belong to men late at night. They were doing something that they shouldn't be. Drug running, maybe. Or perhaps preparing an attack. Wazir hadn't been told why he should find the men, only that he should, and he was certain that these were what the Americans were looking for.

Wazir parked up his taxi, turned off his lights, and picked up the phone between his legs. He watched as the four pickup trucks loaded up with men and drove away with no lights turned on. Wazir reported everything that he saw to his handler, then hung up the phone. Too late he saw the two men standing beside his door. Wazir fumbled for the lock, but the other man was quicker. He yanked it open as the second leaned in and grabbed Wazir by his hair.

A heartbeat later there was a knife at his throat, and Wazir knew that his time as a spy was over. Now he must be a father, and a husband, and protect his family.

And so Wazir grabbed the man's wrist, and pushed the blade into his own throat. As he bled to death in the seat of his car, his last thoughts were of Afghanistan, and the future that he had died to preserve.

CHAPTER 71

BAGRAM

Federico Vasquez lit a cigarette and shook his head.

'His handler has been trying to get hold of him for an hour now.' He handed back Powell's Newports to her. 'Nothing after his initial sighting.'

'Do you think they lifted him?' she asked, her face lined with fatigue. Both of the intelligence agents were running on caffeine and nicotine, and now, worry.

'Must have done,' Vasquez replied. 'My guys say that he's solid. Has never let him down. If he's not calling in, something went wrong.'

'Fuck. How much does he know?'

'Only that we were tipped off there was something going down tonight, and that we needed him to be on the lookout.'

Powell thought about it for a moment. 'If he tells them that, it's not a reach for them to figure out what we know about the hostage transfer.'

The American nodded. 'Right.'

'And then Roshan will either use it as a trap, or back out, and Sherali kills the hostages and cuts his losses.'

'Right.'

'Fuck.'

'Yeah.'

'What do you think we should do?' Powell asked him.

'Honestly, I don't know. This is a British-led mission. What do you think?'

Powell didn't hesitate. 'Nothing changes. All we know is what we know, which isn't much. If there has been a compromise and there is going to be an ambush on the team, we'll have warning from the air assets. Then we look at our options. If Roshan pulls out, so what? We are just hours away from the rescue. The ball is rolling no matter what has happened elsewhere.'

Vasquez shook his head. 'If they got him, they're not gonna fuck around with this guy. It will be straight to cutting off pieces of him, and maybe his family too. Fuck. His family ...'

Powell looked at him. 'Can we get them out?'

Vasquez shook his head. He seemed a little disgusted with himself. 'No. It's not ... it's not what we do. If they get compromised ...'

'The family pay the price,' Powell finished for him.

'Yeah.' For a moment Vasquez looked like he was ready to hit something, but he composed himself quickly. 'Sometimes I hate this fucking job, I really fucking do.'

Powell got them back to what mattered. 'We give the teams what we know,' she told him. 'Four pickups and two dozen men seen and possibly heading towards the target. That's a fact. All the rest is speculation. Here.'

She tossed him back her Newports. 'I'll get a new pack later.'

CHAPTER 72

Miller raised his night-vision goggles and looked around him. After more than an hour of hard pushing up the hillside they had cleared the forest and the SEAL didn't need his NVGs to see. The sky was thick with stars and a moon lit up the valley floor and highlighted the rugged mountain peaks. Nowhere could replace his home state of Montana in Miller's heart, but this country came pretty close. If they ever stopped fighting here, valleys like this would be studded by 10-million-dollar mansions, and ski resorts in the winter. Maybe that was one reason why the Afghans kept fighting. Miller could sure as shit understand the desire to keep your home the way it was. That was why he was here in this valley: fighting to preserve his way of life, and the American ideal of freedom.

The man ahead of Miller raised from a crouch and continued to move. He was an SAS trooper, and Miller thought that he moved well at night. Considering most of these Brits came from towns and cities, they'd learned to use the land and traverse it like experienced hunters. When all this was over, and the war was done, Miller hoped that friends like Allen, and now Taff, would come and visit him back home. He knew that they'd love what he had to offer. They could hike the mountains, do some hunting, maybe even get them on the back of a horse. For Miller, war had never been the end goal. He was here so that he could get back to his calling: working the land and raising livestock that would feed both his own family and strangers. He knew that he was a rarity in that respect. A lot of the men on the mountainside with him didn't want the war to end. Operations were their oxygen. When all was said and done, he wondered how many of them could find peace with their new lives. No warrior gets to fight forever. If the enemy didn't put an end to your career, then someone with a pen would.

Miller moved off with a light but quick step.

Up ahead, he caught sight of the snake of men as they wound their way up the mountainside. A team of SAS were leading the way, the men who were to provide the western cut-off group. They were followed by the SAS team that would assault Cave Alpha, then Miller's team, who would now assault Cave Bravo. Finally came the SEAL team that would provide the eastern cut-off. In the middle was a small option command element of Coates and his SEAL JTAC (joint terminal attack controller), who would bring down fire support from their air assets. Miller raised a smile through the sweat as he thought of Allen and Banks being held back with Coates. He must start thinking of some jokes to bust their balls with when this was all over.

All told it was fewer than 45 men. They outnumbered the kidnappers and that suited Miller just fine. There were plenty of dead men who had gone looking for fair fights. Besides, the caves would give the enemy an advantage. On the special forces' side would be surprise and the best training that had ever existed, matched with thousands of hours of operational experience. This was no one's first rodeo. Every man on this mission had been under fire more times than he could count.

Could the enemy say the same?

CHAPTER 73

Shah Roshan looked in the wing mirror of his pickup truck and saw three more following him in the moonlight. Roshan was riding in the passenger seat, as befitted a Taliban commander, and he chose to be in the lead vehicle because he had built a reputation for being at the front of a fight. It was a reputation well earned and one that Roshan was proud of. Men feared him, and that was a good thing. Roshan enjoyed battle. Always had. That was what had made the last few years so difficult.

In 2001, when the Americans came, Roshan and his men had put up stern resistance, holding up a Northern Alliance advance. Then the American jets had come, bombing his men to pieces, and the town where they were making their stand along with them. Roshan saw dozens of dead civilians, children among them. It only strengthened his resolve to fight the invaders until his last breath. He was ready to give his life for God and the Taliban and Afghanistan, but his commanders had other ideas: they ordered Roshan to pull back with the men that he had left. Roshan had expected that they would make Kabul a deathtrap for the invaders, forcing them to destroy the city and show the world who they really were, but instead Roshan and his men were ordered to Pakistan. At first he was furious. He felt that the actions were cowardly, but over time he came to see the wisdom of his commanders' actions. In Pakistan the Taliban regrouped, reorganised, re-equipped, and received thousands of new recruits who wanted to wage jihad against the invaders. His commanders were clever. They were able to drag it out year by year, and in each of those years the Americans and their allies lost men and support in their homelands. Every village that they bombed turn people towards the Taliban. Every coffin sent home made more in their country demand peace. Slowly but surely, the Taliban were bleeding the Americans and their puppet republic to death.

In this time, Roshan and his men were not idle. They had been sent several times to fight in Kandahar and Helmand Province. Roshan had fought against Canadians, Danes, British and the most hated Americans. He had fought Afghans too, and taken great pleasure in beheading the traitors they captured, mounting their heads on sticks as warnings for those who would turn their backs on Afghanistan. Roshan had been shot once and concussed from bombs several times. He had lost dozens and dozens of his men, but they were not to be mourned, rather honoured. What was most gratifying was the number of young men who swelled their ranks. They came from Afghanistan, Pakistan and even, sometimes, from countries like Britain. They had seen the truth of America's evil, and would die to stop it. It made Roshan proud. So very proud. When President Obama announced a timeline for withdrawing all US troops in 2011, Roshan and his men rejoiced. They knew for certain now that the war was won. Even if it took another 10 years, the Taliban would be restored. It was clear.

And so it was with some frustration that Roshan was dispatched to Badakhshan with only two dozen men. They were not ordinary men, of course, but special fighters picked for their bravery and experience. They were being sent to Badakhshan to await special assignments, but all the same, Roshan missed the rush of battle that he had experienced in places like Sangin. Nothing gave him more joy than watching a convoy of the invaders drive into a trap that he had laid, the first vehicle blown to pieces with a bomb, the others then destroyed with RPGs and machine-gun fire. The greatest sight in the world was seeing the invaders' helicopters come in to carry away their dead and dying. Roshan hadn't managed to shoot down a helicopter, not yet, but there was still time. The war was won, but not over.

When Roshan had received news of a special mission, he had been elated. He and his men had been lying low in Fayzabad under the protection of a warlord who pretended to be on the US's side. Instead he was a true believer who provided Roshan and his men with food, lodgings and, now, weapons. Roshan had hoped that these would be used to overrun the invaders' base, even if it meant that they all died in the process. He had men watching it at all times, and they had reported to him that night that six of the enemy's helicopters had left there heading towards Kabul. Roshan wished that he could have been facing them instead of being dispatched on what was little more than a courier run. He and his men had been ordered to take delivery of four women, and bring two of them to Pakistan. The other two he was to throw out onto the streets of Fayzabad without their heads. They would serve as bloody reminders of what happened to

Afghan women who sided with the enemy. Roshan was glad of this. It had been some time since his men had killed, and like every skill, the practice of being hard had to be practised. The women would not have quick deaths. He would make sure that each of his men participated in the killing, blooding them as a master does with his hounds. That was how Roshan had been taught himself, on prisoners. Each man would take an ear, or a finger, or an eye, or a toe. That was why all had taken part in the death. It made a man tough, and a man must be tough to fight a war even if their enemies were soft, like the ice cream they liked so much.

Roshan leaned forward and peered into the sky. The stars were bright and beautiful, a blessing from God. He then lifted a pair of night-vision goggles to his eyes and scanned the landscape. As always, he enjoyed the irony that these goggles had been provided to the Pakistani military as part of US aid to the country. From there, like so much other equipment, weapons and ammunition, they found their way into the hands of America's bravest enemy. It always made Roshan smile to know that America was paying to kill its own troops. And yet somehow they claimed to be the moral masters of the world.

'How far, boss?' his driver Gul asked. The man had leathery skin and a thick beard. He had been by Roshan's side for years, and killed many men. Roshan was proud to have him. He was proud of all his men. They were only two dozen, but he claimed that few Taliban commanders could boast such experienced and brave fighters as he did.

'Another two hours,' Roshan said. 'If we don't stop.' He knew these lands better than his own children. 'The sooner we get these women to Pakistan, the sooner we can be sent into a fight.'

His driver smiled. For Roshan's men, nothing was more glorious than combat against the invader. None of them knew that in a few hours' time, they would have their wish, and more.

CHAPTER 74

Since becoming a soldier, Taff had heard the saying that 'no plan survives contact with the enemy' thousands of times. It was two hours after dismounting the Black Hawks that Murphy's Law was once again proved true.

Technically it wasn't the enemy that caused the change in the rescue plan but the ground itself. That was nothing new. In the Falklands, natural features like the Fortuna Glacier had caused more damage to the SAS missions than the enemy had. Weather could kill you as easily – often more easily – than any enemy fighter, and the terrain of Afghanistan was treacherous.

Taff had been looking straight ahead at the men in front of him when he saw the mountainside rock crumble beneath an operator from the western cut-off. One second they were patrolling silently, the next a body was tumbling down the mountain like a bowling ball.

Taff was the first one to get to him, sliding downwards and controlling his descent with one gloved hand while holding his weapon high and clear of dirt and debris with the other. The treeline below had mercifully caught the man and stopped him from falling any further. It was a small mercy, though, as the impact of the trees had been hard and heavy. He was grunting hard against the pain. When Taff saw a leg at an unnatural angle it was clear how hard he was working not to shout out in pain.

'Hold tight,' he told him. 'You want morphine?'

'Fucking right I want morphine,' he answered through gritted teeth. 'Cunt. Fucking cunt. Fuck.'

Taff understood the pain that was behind the words. It wasn't the broken bone that was causing the trooper to say it, but the knowledge that his mission and tour were now over.

Coates and his JTAC arrived beside Taff just as he was plunging the morphine autojet into the casualty's good thigh. Once off the Black Hawk, the JTAC never left the ground commander's side. Air support could be needed at any time.

'This is what's going to happen. The teams will move on, and you will remain here and grizz it out. I'll leave two as protection and get you stabilised. A heli will lift you as soon as it goes noisy. You understand?'

The operator was just seconds away from sedation but Coates got what he wanted, an acknowledgement.

Taff felt a rising panic inside himself, fearful that his quick actions were about to cost him his own place on the assault. Relief flooded over him as Coates made his decision and wanted Taff to action it.

'Get one man from each of the two assault teams.'

'Roger, boss.' Taff got to his feet. 'And what do you want to do about replacing these two on the assault team?'

CHAPTER 75

'Roger that,' Allen said into his sat phone. 'Do you want the good news or the bad news?' he then said quietly to Banks.

'Just fucking tell me.'

'One of the cut-offs is down with a CAT B,' Allen told him, meaning that they were stretcher cases but not critical. 'Two assaulters have been left behind with him.'

Allen waited to see if Banks would have something to say about that, but the SEAL said nothing.

'So what's the good news?'

Allen let him dangle for a moment before he said it. 'We need to start collapsing the OP,' he told the SEAL. 'We're not just going to take them to the start lines, we're going in with them. I got Cave Alpha, you got Bravo.'

For a moment Banks couldn't believe what he'd heard. Allen felt the same, but he tempered the surge of excitement with the knowledge that his opportunity had come at the cost of an injury. He was relieved to know that neither man was critically injured, but still, the thought of four operators being left behind, even temporarily, was not a comfortable one.

CHAPTER 76

BAGRAM

Vasquez shook his head in admiration when Powell received the latest from the team on the ground.

Powell agreed, looking over her notes. 'The observation post team are collapsing. They're joining the assault teams. At least there'll be two smiles on the ground.'

'Pros have egos.'

'No doubt, but that ego is based on delivering, so first they'll deliver.'

CHAPTER 77

It was deep into the early hours when the teams crested the final ridge and began to drop into the valley that housed the two target caves. Allen and Banks waited silently for them to RV at their now closed-down OP position.

Allen saw the first of them approaching through the trees, moving like silent ghouls in a haunted forest. Pritch, in the front, was short and stocky, but was so light on his feet he might want to take up ballet after the army. He moved forward towards the RV with the OP team with his arms outstretched and his weapon in his left hand. That was this op's confirmation that the group coming towards Allen and Banks were the team. Behind Pritch came Ricky, tall and slender like a flagpole, with a long, rangy gait. The approaching men's night vision appeared like green eyes, dozens of them creeping through the forest that might have been a thousand years old, or older still.

Allen flashed an IR torch in Pritch's direction. The lead scout acknowledged it by giving Allen a thumbs up. He came to a stop beside him and took a knee.

'Miss me, darling?' he whispered.

'How is the lad that went down?' Allen asked back.

'Stable. He'll be all right, just pissed off to miss this.'

'Any dramas other than that?'

'Nah, mate.'

'You sure?' Allen asked quietly. 'I can hear the sweat dripping off you.'

'Some of us work for a living, mate. Not mincing about with buckshee parachute insertions.'

The two figures of option command came towards them in the dark.

The JTAC and Coates took a knee beside Allen.

'All right, boss?'

'All good. Anything you need to update us on?'

'No movement, boss. Anything from the drones?'

'No, nothing from them either.'

'Okay. I'll bring the team commanders in now. Can you orientate us to the ground from here?'

'Definitely, boss. You bring any snipers? This is a good position.'

'The SEALs did. I'll have their sniper pair come up.'

'Nay dramas, boss.'

More figures emerged from the darkness as the two assault team leaders and two cut-off team leaders appeared from the forest and gathered on Allen's position. He heard the two SEALs exchanging words as Banks briefed the snipers. They were at a distance of more than four football field lengths from the caves, but every word was low and slow. Sound travelled a long way at night, even with the shroud of the forest to cloak it.

'Okay, Al,' Coates said when everyone had gathered. 'Take us through it.'

As a young soldier, Allen had been taught how to give target indications, and how to describe what was in front of him based on features, distances and axes. It was an important part of a soldier's training, but there was a much simpler way of doing things these days.

Allen brought his weapon up to his shoulder and used an IR laser to paint what he was pointing at. The beam was visible to the operators through their NVGs.

'That's Cave Alpha's entry point,' Allen said.

Allen turned the laser off, then repainted it on another part of the valley some 200 metres east of the original cave. 'This is Cave Bravo's entry point,' he said. The SEALs' target.

'Any idea which hostages are in which cave?' one of the American team leaders asked.

'No. We couldn't make a positive ID through thermal or NVGs.'

'Okay.'

He turned to the cut-off commanders as the two snipers checked their arcs of fire to make sure they could see both targets through their optics; just as importantly, that they also had muzzle clearance from the rocks immediately in front of the weapon so they could fire without the rounds hitting an obstacle a metre ahead. Their optics were mounted higher than the barrel, and if muzzle clearance wasn't checked, the optic could be looking over the obstruction and the muzzle facing it.

'Start moving your teams into position.'

Coates was clock watching and needed to crack on.

As the rest stayed still, the two cut-off commanders slowly stood up and Coates watched the two men disappear back to their teams before he turned back to the OP team.

'Get us to the start lines.'

CHAPTER 78

Umid couldn't help but think that his turns on watch lasted longer than the other men's and that his time to sleep vanished in an instant. This night had dragged on even longer than the others as Daler had decided that instead of two men standing watch together, one man would guard the cave mouth while one watched the women and the others slept. Daler was usually one of the others. He seemed to sleep a lot. Umid was envious of that.

He was tired, and in truth, he was irritable. The more he thought about 'the test' of shooting Tasneem, the less it seemed like a trial, and the more it seemed like a good reason for Daler and the others to have a laugh at his expense. That was one of the reasons why he had hit Tasneem: she had been a part in his embarrassment, even if an unwitting one. The other reason was because when she looked at him he felt as though he was a child again and explaining himself to his disappointed parents. Well, let her be disappointed, as long as she knew who was in charge, and that was him. Part of Umid wished that Sherali had just given the order to kill the two Afghan women. God willing, they would be rid of all of them by tomorrow, just like Sherali had said.

Umid frowned. He suddenly needed to relieve himself, and Daler had not given instruction about where this should be done. In the other cave there had been space enough to piss without stepping out of the tunnel mouth, but this cave was smaller, and Umid worried that his flow would run across the room and touch one of the other men for which they would surely beat him. And so, Umid decided to break Sherali's rule.

He stepped outside.

CHAPTER 79

The two assault teams and option command were still one group as they snaked closer to the caves. Allen and Banks were up front, leading the way to the start lines. Soon the teams would split and Allen and Banks would move with their own teams to their start lines as quietly as they could, using the ground as cover. Option command would stay static in a position to command and control. The plan had changed twice since the teams were on the helipad at the FOB, but so what? The mission statement hadn't.

'Stand by. Sierra has movement outside Cave Bravo. Cave Bravo.'

The SEAL sniper had the reticule of his optic on the centre of mass of a bandit who had walked sheepishly out of the cave.

Coates stopped to reply and the two teams behind him copied. They didn't need to know why he had stopped; if there was a problem ahead, they'd soon know.

'Is he aware? Over.'

'Negative, looks like he's just taking a piss. You want him down? Over?'

Having the enemy so close didn't mean they were a threat if they didn't know they were in danger. It was the same principle when dealing with enemy fire: just because it's being fired at you doesn't mean it's effective and that you have to stop an advance. It's only effective when the rounds are thudding into the ground about you or people are dropping.

'Negative. Just keep eyes on. If he stays out and sees us, down him before he can get back in the cave. Out.'

The sniper smiled and tapped his friend on the shoulder. 'Looks like we might get in on the action after all.'

And across the valley floor, the young bandit stared at the sky, oblivious that his death was only a trigger pull away.

CHAPTER 80

Laura Jones lay on the blankets that did little to insulate her from the cold ground of the caves. Adele was curled beside her, the Kenyan twitching in a nervous sleep. Laura dared not wake her. It wouldn't be fair to bring her from a bad dream into a worse reality.

When they were first taken hostage – in what felt like years ago, but was probably only a few days – Laura had been optimistic. They had been taken alive and they were unmolested. Her NGO insisted that all members going into the field took a seminar on the dangers of kidnapping, and Laura had been told that the moment of capture was often the most dangerous. The kidnappers might get spooked by something they hadn't expected, and become violent, or they may have come into the situation looking to be violent in the first place. Not all kidnap was for ransom. Some was to rape, and torture, and murder. When none of these had happened to Laura or her friends, she had dared to hope that they would spend a few uncomfortable and admittedly nerve-wracking days in captivity before a ransom was paid and they were released.

The first sign that this was not to be so was the mock execution of Tasneem. The women had been dragged by their hair and slapped and punched but, still, none had been killed, and Laura had convinced herself that the violence had been necessary to get the women to look terrified enough in the video that a ransom would be paid, and soon.

But that hadn't happened, and now, Tasneem and Zahab had been separated from her and Adele. What did this mean? Was something awful happening to the two Afghan women, or were the kidnappers simply playing mind games to try and break their spirit? After all, they can't have liked how Tasneem had stood up to them, unflinching in the face of their mock execution. Could it be that a ransom had been paid for the two Afghan women? Laura knew, with some shame, that this was unlikely. It was always the Westerners that were ransomed first.

And then another – terrible – thought hit her. What if they hadn't been ransomed, but sold? Sold as wives. Sold as workers. Sold as sex slaves. All were possible and the thought of each made Laura feel sick.

She tried not to dwell on it. She tried to hold on to good memories, like the smiling boys playing football in the village that had treated them with such kindness and generosity, but the weight of their reality was crushing, squeezing the air from her lungs and the hope from her heart.

For the first time, Laura began to believe that she would die in this cave.

There was movement in the cave entrance. It was the leader, a black-hearted bandit and a scary man to look at. The weak electric lights of the caves cast long shadows across his cragged face.

Laura mustered her courage.

'Where my friends?' she tried in her best Dari.

He looked surprised to hear his native tongue.

'Where my friends?' Laura said again, stronger this time.

'Alive,' the bandit replied. He could see that she didn't understand this, and so he gave the gesture that Americans were so fond of: a thumbs up.

She stared at him, doubting his words, and the bandit shrugged, as though it were no care of his if she believed him or not. Of course, Laura knew, it wasn't. He held all of the power here.

For the first time she realised that he had something in his hand. He tossed it to her.

It was a chocolate bar. 'Thank you,' she said automatically, regretting the words immediately. She had nothing to thank him for. He was taking everything from her.

'Eat,' he said.

Laura recognising the word broke off a third, leaving the rest in its wrapper beside Adele, ready for when she woke up. The bandit seemed to like that gesture and smiled his piratical smile.

He looked at her for a long moment, and she tried to read what was in his eyes. She couldn't.

'Let me go,' she said in English. 'Let us all go.'

He stared.

'Let us go home.'

He stared. And then he spoke …

'No,' he said in English. 'There will be no home for you.'

CHAPTER 81

Sherali left the woman and went to sit in a quiet part of the cave, away from the noise and stink of the chugging generator. Though in a separate chamber, the stink had made its way into every part of the system. Sherali knew it was a bad, dangerous idea to have it inside, but having it spotted by an American drone would be worse, and they needed the light. The last thing he wanted was for special forces to slit their throats in the darkness.

Sherali worried about such men. It was one of the reasons why he could not sleep. The Russian Spetsnaz had given him many sleepless nights in their war. The things that they would do to prisoners were as bad as what the mujahideen would inflict on the Russians that they caught, and though the Americans and their British allies weren't quite so openly brutal, everyone in Afghanistan knew about prisons like Bagram, and the way that men simply vanished.

The bandit leader was no fool. He knew that the Westerners would be looking for their hostages, and that if they found them they would send their best warriors, often with their dogs. God be good, Sherali hated dogs.

He did not hate the hostages. God willing, the ransom would have been paid, Jallah released, and the women returned unhurt, but the Afghan Republic and their puppet masters had been unwilling to deal. Sherali took no pleasure in sealing the women's fate by selling them to the Taliban, but he would take less pleasure still in failing his boss. And so, the women would be sold, and likely they would be beaten, tortured and eventually killed.

Sherali sighed. It was a hard world.

The old mujahid felt something in his gut. He quickly dismissed the idea that it could be guilt, for he had none, not over this. It was worry, he realised. Worry about NATO's special forces, and about the Taliban who were coming to buy the women. He trusted neither and was wise enough to have fear of both.

Within a second, Sherali made a decision.

'Get up,' he told two of his sleeping men. 'You're going outside.'

CHAPTER 82

'Sierra: That's Cave Bravo now clear. He has gone back inside, still unaware. Wait …'

That was the magic word: no one was to get on the net until the sniper call sign had finished saying what he needed to.

'… That's two bandits now outside Cave Alpha, armed and now moving to their right, away from the cave, but unaware. Over.'

'Roger that. Out.'

As far as Coates was concerned, they could walk wherever they wanted. If they came across one of the teams it would be the last time they walked anywhere. Nothing would stop the attack now.

Both snipers kept their thermal optics to their eye, giving each target just a little lead on their aim as they followed the two bandits about the area. Their weapons were in their hands, but they didn't move like the ghostly SF figures they were unaware were all about them. For a start their only night vision aid was the ambient light from the moon and stars. Both men were lightly equipped, with AK-47s in their hands and chest rigs that would contain the spare magazines. Nothing about the men's demeanour suggested that they expected imminent contact. They were both walking at

---

once, not covering each other's bounds, and they were close together, probably so that they could talk. But even so, the sniper now had an idea what they were outside for.

'Sierra still has the two bandits in the general area of Cave Alpha, no piss, no smoking – it's a possible clearing patrol. Over.'

'Roger that, Sierra, wait …'

Coates took a few seconds to work out what needed to be done.

'… All call signs. If you get compromised, stop it from going noisy. If it does before the assault teams reach their start lines, all call signs are to fight through. Out.'

Coates's thought process was clear, and his order concise. If any team thought they were to be compromised by the clearing patrol, they were to kill them – with a suppressed weapon, a knife, even their bare hands, it didn't matter as long as the valley stayed quiet. But if the compromise did go noisy, the cut-offs would push on to their positions and the attacks on both caves would happen from wherever the two assault teams were on their approach to their start lines. Their surprise would be lost, but not their speed or violence of action.

CHAPTER 83

The snipers were back on the net once more. 'That's the bandits now unsighted between Alpha and Bravo, repeat unsighted between Alpha and Bravo. Over.'

Coates once again stopped and slowly went down on one knee and the assault team copied. 'Roger that, Sierra. Out.'

It took just a couple of seconds for him to make his command decision, as a ground commander has to. Make it, and get on with it. Too much thinking gets people killed.

'Op call sign on me. Out.'

Allen and Burns slowly turned back from the front of the snake to kneel close to Coates and listen in.

'I don't know what those two fucks are doing. It could be just a clearing patrol – maybe being pushed forward to give early warning. Or they could have joined more in that dead ground.'

The two men knew what was coming.

'The snipers can't do anything so you two will push forward and see what the fuck is happening. If you can deal with it yourselves, deal with it. If not, get back here and I'll assess. We need to crack on. I want a start line, not a gang-fuck to get to it. Okay?'

Both men nodded and started to slowly remove their helmets and plates.

CHAPTER 84

Allen and Banks moved towards the dead ground, armed with their suppressed pistols and blades, just as when they had entered the cave. The difference now was that they were without body plates and helmets.

They took short bounds, stopping every few paces to cock an ear in the direction they were heading, mouths open and holding their breath to cut out sounds made by their own swallowing and breathing.

Like most soldiers in the modern era, Allen had never killed with a blade.

The SAS had rammed blades into the necks and chests of German and Italian enemies in the deserts of Africa. During the Falklands War SAS fighting patrols had fought using two-pound ball hammers. One sharp blow to the skull and Argentinian trench sentries would drop silently so that patrols could climb into their trench lines and capture officers for intelligence.

It happened, but it was rare. Very rare. All the same, it was still something Allen had trained for, and knew he had the intention within him, the capability to kill in such a way, and not hesitate to do it. Many soldiers from all armies do not have that intention. A Close Quarter Life Threatening Encounter, as the military call it to make it sound not as serious as it is, has an immense effect on the will of a soldier to kill. That's why armies try to create an emotional distance between their own troops and the enemy. Calling them the Hun, eyeties, gooks, terrorists and, for this conflict, insurgents and bandits reinforces the idea that the enemy is different and so inferior to themselves, the good guys. The Gurkhas' tradition of honour worked for them when it came to killing close up. Once their kukri, a machete-like blade, was drawn, it could not return to its sheath without drawing blood. But Allen wasn't a 19-year-old infantry private any more. He knew he would kill with a blade not because they were bandits and therefore inferior beings, but because he was doing his part to keep all team members safer than they might be if he and Banks didn't sort out whatever danger lay in the dead ground.

For all that, he still hoped he didn't have to use his blade. Man-on-man encounters are never like the films, where the bad guys never fight back and always end up dead. In the real world, it takes a while to die. Because of the amount of oxygen required by the brain, there is a large amount of blood in the skull. Some 20 per cent of blood from the heart flows to the brain, and that has to be stopped to keep the target from screaming out while you're killing them. The problem is, there is always a chance that you fuck it up and become the one that's dead.

It was hard work which required a cool head, but the same could be said for most of an operator's work. Allen had killed with his rifle and his pistol, often close enough to hear the man's last breath. Tonight, hopefully, his suppressed pistol would do the work for him.

As they inched closer, the OP team could just make out the bandits' mumblings. They reached the rocks that divided them and the dead ground and both men lay and listened. The mumblings had developed into low-tone talking that anyone in any language could make sense of. The two voices were bored and tired.

Banks was closer to the last of the dividing rocks and gently crawled around them to get a look at what they were dealing with. Two might be talking, but that didn't mean there weren't more. He returned and lifted a hand out of the dust to show Allen two fingers, then used them to indicate they were smoking. This was not an ambush; the bandits were not aware. Why they were out of the cave, it didn't matter; they were in the way and could compromise the attack, and Coates wanted them dealt with.

Allen looked at Banks's hands. He was now gripping his tomahawk. Allen silently drew his own fighting knife from its sheath. Banks had had eyes on the targets and he had chosen his weapon. Maybe Banks was worried about any ricochets from their 9mm suppressed – not just because it would be a danger to them, but also because the noise of a round spinning into the air could compromise them. But it really didn't matter why Banks had made his decision; the important thing was that he had. This wasn't the time to think and debate, it was time to take action.

Allen and Banks got up on their feet and inched towards the end of the rocks. They would get as near as they could using the cover, and then sprint the last couple of metres at their targets and kill them. Surprise, speed and violence of action.

Banks was in front, so whoever he attacked Allen would go for the other. It was as simple as that; the less complicated the action, the more effective it would be.

As they drew closer Allen could hear the two Afghans talking even more clearly now and the smell of tobacco filled his nostrils.

He saw Banks check the grip on his tomahawk and the next thing he knew, the American had started running. Allen followed, round the other side of the rocks.

There was a look of confusion in the bandits' eyes and then delayed disbelief about what was happening in front of them. These things are present in a target's head for only a second or two but long enough for them to not shout or get their fingers on triggers.

Allen took long strides and closed the final space, passing Banks who was already bearing down on his target.

Allen pushed against his target, who was still trying to get up onto his feet and grab his weapon. With both legs either side of the bandit Allen collapsed onto his chest. Allen smelled the sweat, tobacco and spice from his last meal as he forced his forearm into the man's mouth, leant into it and rammed the blade into the side of his neck.

Allen couldn't be sure yet if he had severed his carotid artery but that didn't matter. He had control of the body below him. He stabbed again, leaving the double-edged blade in this time, moving it back and forth until his hand was warm and wet as the bandit's heightened heart rate pumped blood from his artery even faster.

Now all Allen had to do was wait for the muffled moans and senseless struggling to stop. It wasn't long before the bandit lay still and Allen heard a *thwack* beside him. He turned and saw Banks pulling his tomahawk out of the second bandit's skull. By the look of the wounds, that was also his second hit.

Allen stood wiping the bandit's blood from his hands onto his trousers, and all the time listening for any reaction from the caves.

The two men stood for another couple of seconds in the silence and then turned and moved back towards the assault teams.

All was good.

CHAPTER 85

BAGRAM

Powell and Vasquez stood at the back of the operations room and watched the Predator drone's feed being played out on a bank of screens. Not for the first time, the British intelligence agent marvelled at American military might and the nation's ability to project power into even the most remote places in the world. Since humans first started fighting each other, they have always developed and used their most advanced technology in war. But for all of the advancements in military technology, the reality on the ground was as hard and brutal as it had ever been. With their hearts in their mouths, Powell and Vasquez had watched the two thermal figures of the special forces operators as they stalked the two patrolling bandits and dispatched them with blades. Where four men had walked, now two were standing. Their victims' still-warm blood was bright in the thermal lenses as it soaked into the dust about their bodies.

Powell and Vasquez were fixed to the screens as the two operators rejoined Coates and the assault teams.

'What's up?' Vasquez asked Powell, reading her expression.

'I just feel useless in these parts,' the Brit replied.

'We did our job, Rach. Now these guys will do theirs.'

'Yeah ... but what about the Taliban?'

Vasquez nodded. 'If they come' – he pointed at the drone screens – 'we'll pick their trucks up. No way they can make it in without being seen, and when they are, we'll light them up.'

The A-10 and an AC-130 Spectre gunship support were all flying high in a holding pattern five minutes' flight from the target area. Any closer would risk alerting the kidnappers that something was going on.

Vasquez turned to the military in the room. 'The injured team. We should have an aircraft in to get them out as soon as it goes noisy in case it's a spicy exfiltration.'

Powell looked around the room. There was tension in the air, and it showed on the faces of the SAS officers and support staff.

'We call it fruity.' She tried to lighten the atmosphere a little but it didn't work.

Powell turned her attention back to the drone screens and watched the snake of operators split in two and make their own way towards their start lines. It was easy for her to know which patrol was which. The SAS were moving to Cave Alpha and the SEALs would hit Bravo. Powell wasn't concerned what hostage was in what cave. The mission was very clear, to rescue the hostages. In 12 years of working alongside JSOC, she had seen just what units like DEVGRU and the SAS were capable of. But that never helped her get over her edginess at not being able to do anything constructive and feeling like a rubbernecker as she watched the action taking over from the planning and preparation.

'Here we go,' Vasquez said quietly, reaching for his cigarettes before putting them away. He had forgotten: no smoking in the ops room. All were peering intently at the screens as the two assault teams crept up to their respective start lines. Powell became aware that her heart was beating faster. This was it. The moment of truth. In the next few minutes there would be death in the caves. She watched intently, almost at the edge of her seat as the two assault teams 'shook out' at their start lines, checking their kit was still secure, their helmet chin straps as tight as could be. Small details matter in the fight. A helmet slipping forward and obscuring an operator's view could mean they are dead by the end of the attack. She listened to the low, almost bored monotone of the team's radio traffic as both cut-offs and assault groups confirmed they were in position. It had to be like that; once you start high pitch, excited, scared or fast radio traffic it is difficult to understand what is being said. Worse still, a fired-up tone becomes infectious and soon no one has a clue what the fuck is being said.

There was a two-second pause on the net as Coates made one last confirmation in his own head that all was good before hitting his radio pressle.

Powell started a prayer that those who paid the price would be the kidnappers, and the kidnappers alone.

Her prayer was cut short as Coates's monotone command almost dribbled out of the ops room speakers.

'All call signs, I have control. Stand by ... stand by ... *go.'*

CHAPTER 86

Allen was number one at the left-hand side of Cave Alpha, and his NVGs were away from his eyes in their helmet mount, both eyes open as they looked down the barrel of his weapon. Drenched in sweat mixed with the bandits' blood, he waited as numbers two and three reached around him and hurled flash-bangs hard into the cave. They had instantaneous fuses. Allen followed straight behind, aiming to make best use of the debilitating effects.

The bright white flashes and heavy thuds of the maroons exploding were intensified inside the cave. To the bandits it would have felt like they were being hit by an air strike. The pressure wave of each detonation bounced off the walls before eventually escaping via the cave entrance. The team felt them as they made entry, but that was good; they were used to fighting through with these things as they created fear and havoc.

Within seconds the first gunshots echoed out.

CHAPTER 87

Everything in Taff's life and career had brought him to this moment. His heart was thumping in his chest as he followed the team into Cave Alpha's mouth, which swallowed them up like a greedy whale.

Taff knew that this was the most deadly moment. The entry point would naturally draw enemy fire because that was the only way into the cave. Even filled with fear and confusion, the bandits could still pull a trigger; all they had to do was get rounds down towards the cave's entrance.

It was no surprise when he took the first corner left into a smaller chamber and saw two bandits, just metres away, still standing with weapons in hands but bent over trying to recover from the flash-bangs. He aimed his weapon at the centre of the nearest man's chest and pulled the trigger.

Click.

The weapon didn't do its job, but the SAS operator did. There was a reason that he and his comrades spent thousands of hours training in Hereford's 'killing house'. Taff's brain had barely registered the stoppage before muscle memory took over. He wasted no time in trying to clear the stoppage. Instead he dropped the weapon, which was held to his body by a sling, and seamlessly drew down his pistol from his chest plate holster and put six rounds into the two men before they had time to react to Taff with their AKs. Within the first five seconds of the boss giving the go, two of the bandits were down and dead.

Another second later and a sledgehammer blow struck Taff in the chest.

'Man down!'

CHAPTER 88

Miller had no idea that his new friend had been hit. He was in his own fight, leading the second assault team into Cave Bravo. DEVGRU tactics were a mirror of those used by the SAS, because flash-bangs make any team's entry safer.

There was a bandit on guard inside the cave, but now he was curled up in the foetal position, eyes screwed tightly closed, his hands covering his ears in an attempt to drown out the noise and flashes. His weapon was beside him but it may as well have been on the other side of the world. Miller wasted no time putting two rounds into the man's chest and a third into his face.

The smell of dust and cordite hit his nostrils. Miller pushed through deeper into the cave, moving to his left to get clear of the entrance as fast as he could, pulling down his NVGs from their helmet mount as he stepped over the leaking body of the man that he had killed. To ensure that white-outs didn't obscure their view, no matter how quickly the NVGs recovered, most operators didn't use their NVGs until the flash-bangs had done their job. Now, through his green night vision, Miller searched for the shapes of men and saw three struggling to get up from where they had been sleeping on the floor, having stayed under their blankets during the flash-bang attack like children in bed blocking out their fear of the dark. He filled them with three-round bursts before they could even get to their knees.

But the last bandit standing was holding Zahab in front of him.

'Let her go! Move away. Now!'

CHAPTER 89

From deeper inside the gloom, a stream of rounds flew down Cave Alpha towards the team. The heavy din of the AK rattled the confined space, and the zing of some of its rounds hitting rock and ricocheting about the confined space underlined the danger to everyone. Some of the rounds passed so close to Allen that he felt the air being displaced by his face. Through his NVGs, now pulled down from their helmet mount, he could see the hung blankets ahead and pushed deeper towards them.

There was no muzzle flash ahead of him from the AK; the firing had to come from the other side of the heavy blankets. In regular close combat he would have fired back through them, but this was a hostage rescue mission. Allen would not see the same result of the Korengal Valley repeated.

He pushed himself hard, deeper into the cave as the AK stopped firing. The weapon's steel mags made an unmistakable noise when being changed for a fully loaded one. From the other side of the blanket wall, Allen could once more smell diesel fumes and hear the chugging generator. He could hear shouts from the bandits he did not understand, and heard female screams of terror that anyone could understand.

With the butt of his weapon in the shoulder and his NVGs pulled up from his face once more, Allen pushed through the heavy blankets and into the weak and yellow glow of the lighting strung along the cave. There was a flash of movement ahead of him that wore a beard and Allen fired a double tap into the centre mass of what he could see of the target. There was a yelp of pain as his rounds made contact, but the target kept on running.

A second later another bandit appeared, letting loose from his AK. Scared – or wanting to help his friend as he took cover? It didn't matter to Allen as he dropped to one knee and drilled two double taps into the man's torso.

The cave was now full of shouts and gunfire, magnified as the sounds had nowhere to go.

Allen edged towards the dropped bandit. He was dead, but the first one wasn't. Allen closed on the generator, the only piece of cover, and found him lying behind the cube of steel. The bandit was trying to make himself as small as he could, his stomach entry wound pushing out dark deoxygenated blood.

Allen gave him a double tap to the head.

A thick cloud of fumes from the chugging generator made him feel light-headed as he checked the instrument panel and jabbed a red button.

A moment later the entire cave system was plunged into darkness.

Now the night vision of the assaulting force came into its own. Allen could hear panicked shouts coming from somewhere as the enemy realised they were cornered, and well and truly fucked.

Allen quickly moved back into the main cavern. He knew where the next chamber was, and what it housed:

The hostages.

CHAPTER 90

Miller kept his aim as best he could on the young bandit who was using Zahab as a human shield.

'Move away guy, now!'

Umid had never been more terrified as he kept Zahab between him and the American.

All Umid could do was shout back in a language that Miller didn't understand, but that didn't matter. What Umid wanted wasn't going to happen in any language.

'Let me go! I'll kill her. Let me go!'

When the flash-bangs had detonated, Umid had wet himself in fear. He knew what that moment must mean, and sure enough, gunshots had followed. All he could think of was staying alive but he couldn't hold Zahab as well as his weapon, so he let that fall to the ground.

He pulled his Choora and held it up to the woman's throat and waited for the inevitable to happen.

He had no doubt that his brothers were dead, Daler among them, and he had equally no doubt that he would soon follow them to the grave.

And yet, some instinct that he did not know he possessed had screamed at him, and given him a chance to survive. Not by fighting, but by placing something precious between himself and the warriors who had come to kill him.

Zahab now joined Umid in the screams, but hers were just dread as he lifted her by the hair to keep her in front of him.

Umid's mind was racing. What to do now?

The shadowy figure in front of him just stood, weapon in the aim, waiting for the opportunity of a clean shot.

Umid's human survival instinct was at full revs, trying desperately to think of positives. Maybe if they didn't let me escape, maybe I would be taken prisoner? Perhaps this was not the end.

But he had forgotten about Tasneem.

CHAPTER 91

Tasneem acted on instinct.

Her head still throbbed from the deafening noise and flashes of light that had had her curling up in the dust, trying to make herself as small as she could as the gunfire filled the whole cave. But now the noise had stopped, and she cautiously straightened herself out.

She found she was behind Umid, who had a knife to her friend's neck. Towards the cave entrance she could just make out the noise-makers and their shouts that meant one thing: it was their rescuers.

And so she acted.

Tasneem felt around for a weapon. She found a rock in the dust. With all of her strength, she raised it above her head in both hands before slamming down onto the back of Umid's head. She felt it connect hard, and the young man was sent staggering sidewards; the blade fell from his hands.

A split second later, Umid's body jerked and spasmed as Miller fired a three-round burst into him. The final round took off the back of his head, spraying Tasneem in brain matter as the young Afghan crumpled to the floor.

Miller lowered his weapon. 'Clear!'

The team ran forward and grabbed the two women. The mission wasn't over until the aircraft had returned everyone to Bagram. Until then the hostages had to be gripped and controlled with hard and clear instructions. If not, they might not do what they were told. Fear could be freaking them out, or their minds might have been scrambled out of the sheer horror of events.

They could put everyone at risk.

CHAPTER 92

As soon as Allen made entry past another wall of blankets covering the hostages' chamber, a hand reached out and grabbed the barrel of his rifle. Allen didn't try and fight it. He let the weapon go, and went for his pistol to end this quickly. But the bandit was quicker and used the weapon on its sling to pull Allen towards him. They both went down onto the floor in a tangle of limbs as the bandit wrestled to get the pistol for himself.

Night vision was useless now. So was all of the technology that Allen had at his disposal. The fighter had done to Allen what Afghanistan did to so many invading armies: dragged the fight down to its most basic and brutal level.

Allen didn't hesitate. He threw his head forward into a savage head-butt and his NVGs crashed into the bandit's face with so many sharp angles.

Allen felt the man reaching for his face, seeking out his eyes. The Afghan's grip was like a vice. He pulled Allen's NVGs off his helmet and Allen felt the first of the man's strong fingers pushing into his eyes. Allen pulled back, buying himself an inch. He threw a vicious right elbow at his assailant in the darkness. Then another. And another. He felt the third one connect with something and heard an angry shout of pain, but the Afghan did not give up.

Both men were wrestling for their lives, and Allen would finish this fight himself.

His left hand pulled the fighting knife from its sheath.

Allen pushed hard and jabbed the blade into the man's side, the Afghan spitting blood as the dagger drove through his kidney. Allen pulled back and jabbed again, and again. The kidnapper made one last desperate attempt to prise out Allen's eyes, but blood was pumping out of his wounds, and he was growing weaker and weaker. Finally, his grip on Allen slacked and Allen pulled free from his grasp to leave the bandit to bleed out. There were more important things to be getting on with.

Hands covered in blood once more, Allen retrieved his NVGs and rolled over to face Laura and Adele. They looked at him, with eyes full of fear.

Allen got to his feet as he looked for his pistol. He wanted movement from the women.

'Get up, now!'

As the women started to comply, Allen's earpiece burst into life.

'All call signs, we have four technicals, manned and inbound from the east. I say again, four technicals, manned and inbound from the east. Out.'

There was a change of plan. 'You two. Get back down and stay there until someone comes for you. You are safe now. Do you understand?'

They stared. Because of fear some people just cannot compute.

Allen pointed down at the dead bandit. It was then that Allen realised the one he had killed was their leader, Sherali.

'He's dead and you are not – if you do what I say. Stay here. Do you understand?'

CHAPTER 93

CREECH AIR FORCE BASE, NEVADA, USA

Sarah Cohen tracked the four technicals that were climbing up the mountain track a few miles away from the special operations forces. Watching the rescue raid go in from the controls of her Predator had been exhilarating, but Cohen had felt like an observer, almost as though she were standing on the sidelines. Now she was a hunter, her drone's optics identifying the Taliban's 12.7mm heavy machine guns mounted on all four vehicles. That was why they were no longer just pickups but technicals. Because of the mounted weapons on each of the flatbeds of these civilian vehicles they were now weapon platforms.

There were two Taliban on the back of each wagon, their legs dangling over the sides. Others were standing up, manning old Russian DShK heavy machine guns. The equivalent of the American .50 Browning, they could penetrate light armour or the engine block of a truck and punch a hole the size of a man's head in a wall at a thousand metres.

These things were the stock weapon for Africa, South East Asia, Iraq and Afghanistan. The Russians started building them in the 1930s to take Vickers' machine-gun ammo, and the Brits donated millions of rounds to them during the Second World War to hammer the Germans. They'd carried on making them until the 1980s. Some donations you live to regret.

Cohen also knew the most important detail about these platforms was that when fired together to create a beaten zone in the air, they could bring down a helicopter. These weapons brought down most of the 7,500 helicopters and fixed-wing aircraft destroyed by Communist forces during the Vietnam War.

The accuracy of her strike was not only vital to the hostages. For this crew, it was the lives of the aircrews and operators that was more important.

Cohen turned to Kerallis, her SWO. 'Range?'

'Four point two kilometres.'

The pilot looked at her instruments: the Predator was at 15,000 feet.

The cameras beneath the drone's nose could work through a 360-degree range of motion, but the Hellfire missiles beneath the Predator's wings required a line of sight to do their deadly work.

'Red Rocks Three,' a voice announced over Cohen's headset, giving her call sign. 'You are clear to engage. Out.'

Cohen looked over at Kerallis, who smiled back. Like a sniper, a drone crew's job usually involved long, long days and nights of surveillance.

The pilot put her drone into a left bank and pushed forward on her controls, dropping altitude. Hitting targets in the mountains was hard work, as the ridges and peaks shortened the line of sight, and closed the window of opportunity to hit the target. The Hellfire had a range of up to 11 kilometres, but for this shot Cohen would close the distance as much as possible. She wanted no more than five seconds from shoot to strike.

Cohen looked across at her SWO's screen. The first technical loomed large as it bounced along the dirt track.

'Painting the target,' Kerallis said. The targeting pod was beneath the drone's nose and worked on a wide axis. Cohen completed her turn so that the missiles could now pick up the 'painted target'.

'Target acquired.' Kerallis used the same monotone in his voice to keep the attack sequence procedural. But today, that was hard for him.

Cohen's own screen was zoomed out so that she could see the mountains and twists in the road. She saw nothing that would obscure the shot. They had the enemy in a kill zone. Now was the time.

'Cleared to fire,' she said calmly.

'Firing now.' Kerallis tried to contain an edge of excitement in his own voice. But it didn't happen, and Cohen gave him a 'you'll make us look bad' stare that made him get a grip. 'Missile away.'

Cohen watched the screen in front of her as the Hellfire raced away from the aircraft, leaving a swirl of vortex in the air.

'Three seconds to impact.' The SWO had finally composed himself. 'Three, two, one, splash.'

Cohen watched as the pickup truck disintegrated on their screens. It was a good kill, and she banked her drone away, clearing the area. Now that the track was blocked by the wreck of the lead vehicle, it was time to make height again and clear the airspace. Coates's JTAC had called in the A-10s, and they needed a clear sky to work in.

CHAPTER 94

Captain Nate Weir of the Texas Air National Guard received word over his radio that the airspace had been cleared, and the convoy of enemy vehicles was stationary and his for the taking. Behind his oxygen mask Weir smiled. If ever there was a man who loved his job it was the pilot of this A-10.

'Thor Two, Thor One. Breaking holding pattern now. Follow me in.'

The A-10 or Warthog was a twin-engine jet aircraft originally designed for taking out tanks, but now was a close air support favourite in the War on Terror.

The mountain peaks vanished quickly behind the A-10s as they flew low, fast and hard across the terrain. Weir had seen almost every part of this country from his cockpit and he'd smoked Taliban from Helmand to Herat. A-10s were an infantryman's best friend, and Weir was proud of that. He was the first to buy a beer for the grunts when he met them at a bar Stateside, and there was nothing more he'd rather be doing in life than pulverising the enemy on their behalf. Today he was supporting a special operations forces raid, which was an honour in itself. Weir didn't worry about letting them down. He was good at what he did. Damn good.

He saw the smoke from the Predator's Hellfire strike and made slight corrections to bring the nose of his aircraft in line with it. Ordinarily, Weir would want to strike a convoy front to back, or back to front, creating a beaten zone along the line of vehicles and maximising the destructive burst from his cannon, but the terrain here dictated that he take the convoy side on. Weir didn't mind that. It meant that he'd get to make at least a couple of attack runs. The massive 30mm Gatling gun under the Warthog's nose was fitted on the aircraft to fire armour-piercing, depleted-uranium rounds for killing tanks. But in Afghanistan, the rounds of choice for Weir and his aviators were high explosive, the same as an Apache used.

The Texan intended on using every bit of his ordnance on this mission. He didn't think the taxpayers would mind.

'I'm taking the rear vehicle,' he told his wingman. 'Follow me in and take the centre of the convoy.'

'You got it,' came the reply.

The sun wasn't far off rising, the distant horizon turning grey, but Weir used his NVGs to sight on the westernmost vehicle. He saw a panicked man running for cover. Too late.

Weir braced himself and let rip. The cannon's recoil was so strong that it almost pushed the aircraft backwards. A familiar noise for all those who had fought in the battlespace of Afghanistan echoed across Badakhshan.

Brrrrrrrtttttttt.

The guttural belch of the rotary cannon was the reason it was simply known as the Warthog.

Dozens and dozens of 30mm high-explosive rounds rained down on the pickup and tore it apart like it was made from wet paper. Weir jinked left then banked right, deploying flares as he went. Behind him, his wingman let his own hell rain down on the convoy. Looking over his shoulder, Weir saw two fireballs explode up towards the sky.

'I'm coming back around,' he told his wingman. 'High angle for combined effects.'

These were the cluster bombs hanging from the Warthog's wings. Once dropped, the bomblets separate from the main casing and spread out over the target area. The bomblets are a mixture of shaped charge, fragmentation and incendiary – effective against the Taliban, who were taking cover, and at the same time ensuring their technical would be destroyed.

Weir climbed into the sky, coming back in on the target higher than he had done from the gun run. There was nothing smart about the bombs under his wing. Weir was attacking old school, like his grandpappy had done against the Nazis. Weir had a lot of instruments at his disposal but he was a gut instinct pilot, with flying in his blood. He could drop this wing ordnance on a bullseye the same way Kobe could sink a game-winning three-pointer.

'Bombs gone, bombs gone,' he said, feeling the G-force pushing him into his seat as he pulled out of his dive. Looking back over his shoulder, he saw the constant flashes of the bomblets detonating along the line of the technicals. The chassis of a pickup truck twirled in the sky. What had been a Taliban force was now chunks of steel and flesh spread across the mountainside. Time to go back to base to rearm and get some breakfast.

'Convoy destroyed,' Weir transmitted over his radio. 'Convoy destroyed. Out.'

CHAPTER 95

The sound of explosions rumbled through the mountains like thunder. Before then had come the distant *Brrrrrrrttttttt* of an A-10's nose cannon. Allen wasn't surprised when he heard Coates on the net.

'All call signs, that's the technicals destroyed. Out.'

That was a relief, but it wasn't the end of the mission. After securing the site, medics had checked the hostages over for injuries. With some worry, Allen had gone back through the caves to check on Taff.

He'd found his friend in good humour as he pointed to the AK strike on his front plate. 'Haven't been put on my arse like that since I got tackled by Sam Warburton.'

'I don't know who that is,' Allen replied.

'That's fucking blasphemy, butt,' the Welshman replied. 'Played him in under-16s. Smashed me he did. My lucky day, isn't it?'

'We're not home yet,' Allen reminded him.

'How are the hostages?'

'All good.'

'And what about you?' Taff looked up and down at Allen and his bloodstained body.

'Not mine,' Allen said, and that was all that mattered.

Coates called in the Black Hawks. The plan was for the cut-offs to stay in position and their lifts would come to them.

The assault teams gripped the hostages and started to march them firmly to the mouths of their respective caves. The sound of Black Hawk rotors gently echoed about the valley. Everyone knew that this wasn't the time to feel the relief of success. That would only happen once back on the pad at Bagram.

The first aircraft came into view, keeping low into the valley.

Then the reason not to feel the relief of success was loud and clear.

From up on the valley's high ground, green AK tracer screamed down on the Black Hawks.

CHAPTER 96

Shah Roshan was angry, but pleased. He was angry because the invader dogs had beaten him and his men to the hostages, and because the explosions in the distance no doubt meant the death of his men that he had sent on the exposed track as a decoy force, but he was pleased because he now had the chance to avenge them, and send the Western pigs to hell.

The Taliban commander hadn't expected to find the invaders in the valley, but like all experienced commanders he had planned and prepared for the unexpected as the Americans were always in the sky.

Roshan had dismounted most of his men from the trucks and led them deep into the mountainside. The bandit leader wasn't the only one to have fought in these mountains against the Russians. Roshan had used the cave and tunnel systems to reach the high ground above the valley, identifying that no one, bandits or the Americans, would know that they were there.

He didn't know the bandits holding the hostages and so he hadn't trusted them. His plan had been to observe the cave from the high ground while sending just a few men with the trucks to check the situation.

The failure of the hostage handover was now irrelevant. God had given Roshan the invaders to kill instead. For God he must kill as many of the invaders as possible. In his heart he knew that this would be his final battle, and he rejoiced at that. There was no higher form of honour than sacrificing yourself for God's will.

Roshan knew that with just his 16 Taliban he was outnumbered, but numbers counted for less when the defenders had the high ground.

Roshan looked at the sun climbing over the mountains. This would be his last dawn, and God had given him a beautiful one to gaze upon while he worked out his plan to start killing. But his thoughts were broken as he heard helicopter rotors below him in the valley.

The Black Hawk was surely a gift from God.

'Fire!' he yelled. 'Allahu Akbar! Allahu Akbar!'

CHAPTER 97

Mel peered down and to her right at the first Black Hawk as Steve Ream dropped height and flew deep inside the valley on his approach to the blue smoke to pick up the Brit assault team and hostages. Just then, her helmet display exposed body-heat signatures splashing out from the rocky terrain on the mountainside above the valley. A split second later, the chain gun was pumping four-round bursts of 30mm HE rounds into her targets, the weapon's distinctive *da-da-da-da* signature filling the sky to let everyone on the ground know shit was on.

'Contact. Contact. Abort now. Abort.'

Her voice was as procedural as the rest of the pilots' as she kept looking down left, down right, up, scanning across the hill, the chain gun below her obediently following her head movements.

Izaak banked the aircraft to face on the hillside. Mel continued to engage on whatever she could see through the banks of dust thrown up by rounds impacting the ground. Ream flew his Black Hawk low and fast through the valley to escape. He didn't need the contact report; two rounds crashing into his cockpit via one of the roof windows told him all he needed to know.

'Mel, I have the pods lined up and making the approach now.'

'Yo, switching now. Going white phos.'

Mel's thumb was on the button controlling the target acquisition and designation system to fire the Hydra white phosphorous rockets.

Through her helmet display she could see the beaten zone she wanted to hit. The attackers were unsighted in there somewhere among the dust clouds.

'Stand by.'

Her thumb pressed down and four Hydra-70s, two from each of the missile tube launchers, whooshed past the crew in sequence, their plumes of black smoke trailing behind them. The fin-stabilised unguided rockets flew for three seconds before making contact; there was a yellow flash initially, before the phosphorus made contact with air and exploded into a blinding haze of white. The hill was covered in an angry cloud that pushed its way under every rock and crevice.

Any humans in its way would now be burning until they were dead.

Ream was on the net. 'Reaper One Four is clear of the valley. Clear now.'

'Roger that, Reaper One Four. Disengaging.'

Izaak banked his aircraft away from the valley as all aircraft swooped out of the area. His two-ships were there to protect the Black Hawks. He needed to conserve ammunition because the operation hadn't ended for them: they still had to get the teams out.

'What you think, Mel? You got 'em?'

'Not sure – those fucking caves.'

• • •

Standing in the valley with his JTAC kneeling beside him, Coates was thinking the same thing as the last of the white phos cloud evaporated and the sound of the Black Hawks' rotors grew dim. There was nothing to indicate that the Apache ordnance had done its job. The caves up there provided good cover, so there could be survivors who could still fight. Coates wasn't going to let that happen. He wanted the pickups in as soon as possible.

'All call signs. I am clearing the high ground. Keep your heads down. Out.'

He tapped the top of the JTAC's helmet as if gently knocking on a door.

'Fire mission.'

CHAPTER 98

High above the province circled the AC-130 gunship. The crew of 13 were long in experience, having supported dozens of special forces ops. The crew was on month five of their year in-country. When the call came, they were ready.

'Fire mission,' the commander said over the crew comms net as she flew the last two minutes to be on target. All the while, JTAC continued relaying the enemy positions to the fire control officer, who sat in front of his battle-management screens. The monitors were situated between the six-barrelled 25mm Gatling gun that was positioned behind the pilots and the 40mm Bofors about halfway down the fuse-lage. The 105 was just a bit further along towards the rear.

As the aircraft approached the target area, the pilot flew in a left orbit. The weapons were all positioned on its left flank, bristling like a battleship, and they now pointed down towards the mountainside. The fire control officer gave each of the weapons crews their targets. A few of them smiled. This was their favourite kind of fire mission: every single weapon at their disposal was going to be employed.

CHAPTER 99

The first indication Roshan had about more enemy aircraft above them came the moment he heard a 105mm shell crash into the mountainside. It didn't explode on impact; there was a delayed fuse to allow it to force its way past the rock. The thunder of the explosion came three seconds later, obliterating two of his men to add to the toll taken by the mosquitoes. Moments later, streams of bright red tracer were falling from the heavens. With his own eyes, Roshan saw more men killed, cut to ribbons by the unending stream of rounds descending on them from the six-barrel Gatling gun. As they struck the ground there was another 105 detonation, the combination of ordnance kicking up another thick fog of dust almost impossible to see through. But as another 105 shuddered into the hillside, Roshan knew the Americans would be able to see. The Taliban commander watched as the remainder of his men were cut down like dogs by the cowardly Americans in the sky.

As Roshan scrambled towards a cave, his ears filled by the screams of the dying, he looked back to see Gul just metres behind him.

'Come! Hurry! The caves!'

But his old friend and driver, the last of his men, didn't even have time to move before being ripped apart from the detonation of the Bofors 40mm rounds.

The cowardly invaders would not kill Roshan like a dog. To do that, they would have to fight him like men.

CHAPTER 100

Allen watched in awe as streams of red tracer fell from the sky like laser beams. The Spectre gunship's fire mission looked like something out of a science fiction movie, explosions pulverising the mountainside as the last 105 crashed into the hillside and the AC-130 broke off its orbit.

End of mission. No one could be expected to live through such a bombardment.

Behind him, he heard the pop of a smoke grenade as it pumped out its blue.

CHAPTER 101

Shah Roshan was about to leave the world a hero.

He was now lower down the valley, so close to the invaders. After scrambling through tunnels and caves, flashes of past glories killing Russian invaders from these very rocks pulsating through his brain, he felt a final surge of energy for the fight that lay ahead. It was as if he no longer had control of his body, that God was helping him along the path to win more glory and so join him in paradise.

Roshan lay among the rocks, soaked with sweat, watching and listening. Invaders were scattered about the caves' entrances, dragging the bandits' bodies outside and taking their photos and fingerprints, and using their radios as blue smoke rose into the sky.

It wasn't long before once again a Black Hawk's rotors gently started to fill the valley and Roshan began moving closer to the caves. Soon he would go to paradise, while the invaders would forever suffer the torments of hell.

The Taliban commander pulled the long blade that he had used to behead a dozen men. What better gift to God than the head of an invader?

Roshan crawled closer to the back of his nearest target, and ran the last two metres at him.

He threw his left hand around to grab at the invader's helmet as the right clenched the blade that would sweep across the invader's throat, then cut through to his spine and separate his head from his shoulders.

The Talib felt the thrill of religious enlightenment as he came into contact with his enemy.

And almost immediately, he felt something strike him twice. He fell backwards.

The last thing that the Taliban commander ever saw was Allen's pistol pointed at his face, and Banks, the invader that Roshan was so close to beheading. He had just enough time to smile at the thought of being with God before Allen pulled the trigger.

Allen holstered his weapon while Banks took a moment to think about what might have been. His thoughts were broken by a slap down onto a shoulder by Allen as the arriving aircrafts' rotors pitch changed and they prepared to land.

'Come on, let's fuck off.'

CHAPTER 102

BAGRAM

Powell and Vasquez watched as the four Black Hawks came over the horizon. First they were tiny specks, then the sound of the rotors grew louder and the four helicopters came in and landed in an impressive formation, their wheels touching the ground of Bagram Airbase almost simultaneously.

A small crowd had gathered to watch the return of the victorious hostage rescue team. The UK ambassador was surrounded by his entourage, along with several officers. A number of other officers who had nothing to do with the operation but wanted to be part of it in some small way were also there; otherwise, what else would there be to tell their kids about?

Ambulances and their crews were stationed at the edge of the HLS ready to take the wounded operator to the base hospital, and the hostages too. No doubt the women would be dehydrated as well as traumatised and needed to be checked out.

Powell and Vasquez would go with them to extract whatever intelligence they could while it was still fresh in the women's minds. In the intelligence game, you never knew what would go towards building the bigger picture. The hostages may have seen or heard something that could prove to be a clue in solving the bigger picture of Afghanistan's web of criminal and terrorist enterprises.

The violence had ended, and it was now once again Powell and Vasquez's war.

Vasquez pulled out a near empty packet of Newports and offered it to Powell. 'Victory cigar?'

'I don't think we're supposed to smoke here,' she said as she took one before pointing at the aircraft.

Vasquez lit them both and took a few happy puffs. 'This is the good part,' he said, blowing out a cloud. Together they watched the Apache two-ship land onto another pad of the HLS. But then his smile evaporated.

Powell knew what he was thinking. 'The asset?'

Vasquez nodded. 'Wazir, a young guy. No one will ever know it, but he died for these hostages.' He blew another cloud of smoke. 'That's how it goes in this war, isn't it? We know the names of our guys who died. Or at least, they flash it on the news for a moment, back home, but no one knows how many Afghans have died for this mission. The big mission, I mean. For every one of our guys, dozens of Afghans have paid the price. I just wish that people knew that.'

'We do,' Powell said. 'And maybe that is enough.'

'Maybe,' the American replied, forcing a smile back on to his face. 'But hey, this is a good moment. It's a win, and you've got to celebrate those when you can.'

He held out a clenched fist to Powell. She looked at it.

'Don't be so British.' He laughed. 'Pound it.'

Powell completed her first-ever fist bump as the hostages were being helped out of the Black Hawks.

CHAPTER 103

Safe now, the hostages didn't need to be gripped, they needed to be helped, and the soldier who supported Tasneem down from the helicopter was a fearsome sight.

He had a thick beard and dark, penetrating eyes. There were dark red stains on his gloved hands and splattered across his uniform, and he bristled with weapons: a rifle, a pistol and a blade crusting with dried blood.

And yet the man could not have been more kind or gentle as he helped her down from the helicopter, the rotors of which were slowly coming to a stop, a whine as the engine died. The smell of the airbase hit Tasneem's nostrils. It smelled of gasoline, burning trash and hot dust.

Her feet touched the floor.

'Are you okay?' the man asked her. 'You can hold my arm if you need to?'

Tasneem did not need to, but she did so anyway. She did it for him, because he had risked his life for her, and he deserved to be seen by the people, a mixture of military and civilian, who waited for them. Tasneem had never served in the military but she had operated in several organisations, and they were always the same. When there was good news, people would want to be part of it. Tasneem knew that everyone had a role to fill, but she didn't want this brave man to be overlooked in his.

'Take your time,' the soldier said, and Tasneem smiled at him.

'I expect you want this part over with as much as I do.'

He laughed from behind his face hair. 'Aye. Fair one.'

Tasneem looked around and waved as her three fellow aid workers were escorted by their own knights in not-so-shining armour. Instinctively the men stood aside and let the four women embrace. There were a few tears, but they were relieved ones. Mostly there were only smiles, and looks of incredulity at their surroundings. There was no doubt about it now. They were safe. Truly safe.

Perhaps growing impatient at the delay, the group of officers started walking towards the hostages followed by the ambassador to move events along.

The ambassador held out a hand and a very British handshake took place between the two Brits.

It was easy to know that he was the man in charge. The others took their station from him, a flock of geese in flight, staggered backwards on his flanks. The operation had been a success, so now politics would be taking over.

The ambassador then shook hands with Adele and Zahab before greeting the last of the women.

'You must be Tasneem.'

'I am.'

'I've been told that you helped our men. Thank you,' he said, shaking her hand.

She understood that politics would always want a part in success. But yet she saw in the man's eyes that he was truly relieved and happy to see them safe and well.

'Now,' he said smiling to the group, 'it's a simple medical to make sure you are all okay, then maybe tea with some people who would like to talk with you all?'

CHAPTER 104

There was still work for the teams to do and Coates made sure no one forgot.

'Listen in! Debrief at ...' He checked his watch. 'Eleven hundred. Get fed. It'll be a long one.'

Allen joined the rest of the teams on their way to the unloading bays to clear all weapons. They shook hands, fist bumped, patted each other on the back. Everyone had done their part, and done it well. A true team effort, nothing less.

Allen saw someone approach him from the corner of his eye.

'You look like you could use a powerwash,' Banks told him.

'You need to check yourself, mate.'

For a long time the two men stood in silence, taking in the scene.

'These are the moments,' the SEAL said at last, 'these are the ones we'll remember for the rest of our lives.'

Allen allowed himself a little grin. 'You lot, you're fucking cheesy.'

Banks laughed. 'Spoken like a true Brit. Where's your tea?'

'Where's your eagle? I thought we'd be having a fly past and some fireworks or something.'

'Had enough of those for the day, I reckon. Hell of a fight.'

'Aye, it wasn't a bad one, was it?'

Banks grinned as he surveyed the joint force of SAS and SEALs.

'We should do this more often.'

'Fuck that. Saving your arse once is enough.'

Allen laughed as he headed to unload. Banks joined him as he finally got the joke.

CHAPTER 105

Vasquez and Powell had stood in the back of the ops room while the SAS troopers and SEALs went through their debrief. With teas and coffees in hands, and sweat and grime on their faces, the operators went through the mission step by step, detailing what had worked, what hadn't, who had done what, and where. It was this collation of information that allowed them to get better day by day, mission by mission. They were living proof of the special forces ethos: the unrelenting pursuit of excellence.

Powell and Vasquez shared a look as the briefing finished and they left the room. 'I'm glad they're on our side,' Vasquez said with a smile. The men were tough, and rugged, and though they sat in the briefing room as quiet professionals, there was no doubt that they were brutal men when they needed to be.

Powell climbed into Vasquez's pickup truck and they drove to the base hospital. After stopping in quickly to see the wounded SAS operator, the two intelligence agents met with the hostages. The four women had been gathered in a room. It was the oldest, an Afghan, who greeted them with a smile.

'Hi,' she said. 'I'm Tasneem.'

'I'm Fede.' He held a smile and addressed the group. 'And this is Rachael. We'd like to talk to you all, if you don't mind?'

Though the questions were directed at the group, it was Tasneem who did most of the answering. Both agents were impressed by the detail which she recounted. She'd picked up names, and recalled conversations about towns, stories that she'd overheard from the men who had been guarding her. It was clear that she had been proactive as a hostage, not giving into her situation but attempting to master it.

'This is all very helpful,' Powell said with admiration. 'Very, very helpful.'

'I feel like I should offer you a job.' Vasquez smiled.

Tasneem smiled back. 'Thanks, but I'm happy doing what I do. When do you think we can be released?' she asked then. 'I'd like to get back to work.'

The agents were taken aback.

'You've been through a lot,' Vasquez told her. 'It's probably a good idea to rest up here for a while.'

Tasneem smiled again. It was a disarming smile. 'Thank you, but the children we help don't have hospitals like these. I would like to get back to them as soon as possible.'

When the two agents walked outside, Vasquez shook his head. 'Damn ...' was all he could say.

'She was something, wasn't she?' Powell said.

Vasquez nodded. 'And I thought our operators were tough.'

He unlocked the pickup and opened the door. 'Come on,' he said. 'This last stop's going to be one chunk of fun.'

CHAPTER 106

Jallah looked up from his shackled hands as the cell door opened and the two agents walked inside. As soon as he saw that they were smiling, his own vanished, replaced by the desperate look of a trapped animal. Then he saw a large file that was held in the American man's hand, and a glimmer of hope returned.

'My release papers?' he asked in Dari.

'Not quite.' Vasquez grinned. He reached inside the file and began to throw glossy photos onto the floor. As each photograph landed, Jallah grew more and more pale.

'We'll leave you with these,' Powell told him.

'Yeah,' Vasquez agreed. 'Spend some quality time with your friends, Jallah.'

They walked towards the door, leaving the bandit looking at the 12 dead faces of the men who had kidnapped on his behalf.

Vasquez stopped on the threshold and turned back with one final retort. 'You can keep those, buddy.' He smiled. 'And we'll keep you.'

CHAPTER 107

The teams were back in the briefing room that evening but this time it wasn't for any brief or debrief. Cans of Bud lay on the tables. The US military's General Order No. 1 banning alcohol didn't apply to civilians, and Powell and Vasquez were just that.

The room was filled with laughter as men recounted stories past and present. A sense of humour was a vital ingredient for anyone fighting against the odds, and adversity – so much so that the Royal Marines even made it a part of the commando ethos.

'Gentlemen!' Powell called out across the room. 'If I may have your attention please – we have a satlink from London.'

The bureaucrat sat in the same chair with the same white wall as background. This time he was dressed formally.

'Gentlemen, the prime minister wishes to congratulate you all on a job well done and to give you his most sincere thanks on behalf of the British people. To our American allies, you risked your own lives for a British citizen, and this will not be forgotten. This mission has demonstrated once again the unbreakable bond that exists between our two nations and between our special forces. JSOC will be remembered by history as one of the most elite fighting forces that ever existed, striking the enemy anywhere, and at any time. The level of cooperation between multinational forces is unparalleled, and will only grow stronger on the back of successful operations like these. Anyway ...' the bureaucrat paused. 'That's the boring part done. I understand that the bar is free so enjoy your evening. You have earned it.'

There was an ironic cheer at that, and the call ended. Allen was glad that it hadn't gone on any longer. He didn't have anything against politicians or whoever that was – he'd be out of work if it wasn't for them – but he wasn't one for listening to them talk, either. Moments like this were rare and needed to be savoured with those who stood the ground.

Taff pushed a can of beer into Allen's hand.

Allen toasted him and drank. Looking around the room and seeing the smiles, he couldn't help but think how different the mood would have been if things had gone just a little differently. But they hadn't. Everyone had come home alive. Some would call it luck. Others would call it the result of rigorous selection, hard training and the unrelenting pursuit of excellence. In Allen's mind, it was a little of all of those.

Across the room, an SAS trooper and a Navy SEAL were engaged in a race to 'shotgun' their beers, using a knife to pierce the can in its centre before drinking it as quickly as possible from the hole. Tonight looked like it might get messy, but celebrating victory and survival was a tale as old as time when it came to warriors.

CHAPTER 108

The next morning, as the sun tipped over the distant mountain summits, Allen nursed a coffee in his hand and a slight hangover in his head. He hadn't put more than a few beers away the night before, but he wasn't much of a drinker, and the altitude of Bagram amplified the effect of alcohol. In a couple of hours he and his squadron would be flying back to Kandahar to continue their deployment, but before they left, he had one last thing to do. He shouldered his magazine grab bag.

Allen found Banks outside of the SEALS' accommodation, sipping his own coffee as he watched the sun come up. The SEAL was having a private moment, reflecting on the couple of seconds when Roshan's knife was about to cut into his neck and he prepared himself for death. He saw Allen approach and got himself back into the real world. He nodded a good morning.

The Scotsman sat beside him, and for a long time neither man said anything. Instead, they watched the blood-red sun fight its way into the sky.

Allen threw the dregs of his coffee into the dust and stood to go. 'Well, that was romantic.'

The American laughed. 'No shit. If you're ever in Bagram, or Virginia Beach, look me up, brother.'

'Same here, mate. Here, a parting gift.'

Allen threw the grab bag down at his friend and walked away.

Banks opened the zip and pulled out Roshan's knife.

GLOSSARY

2i/c – Second in Command

160th SOAR – Special Operations Aviation Regiment. A special operations force of the United States Army that provides helicopter aviation support for special operations forces

A-10 – a US Air Force jet used for close air support in Afghanistan

AC-130 – a heavily armed, long-endurance, ground-attack variant of the C-130 Hercules transport

ACOG – Advanced Combat Optical Gun (sight)

AH-64 Apache – attack helicopter

ANA – Afghan National Army

ANP – Afghan National Police

Army Rangers – the US Army's premier light infantry unit and special operations force within the United States Army Special Operations Command

Bagram – a US base in Afghanistan

Black Hawk – utility helicopter

C-130 – transport aircraft

CENTCOM – Central Command, the US military command responsible for the region that included Afghanistan

CH-47 Chinook – a tandem rotor transport helicopter

CIA – Central Intelligence Agency

CO – Commanding Officer

Cpl – Corporal

CTR – Close Target Recce

Deliberate Option – a planned and prepared assault to rescue hostages

DEVGRU – Development Group, also known as SEAL Team Six

Emergency Response – an assault to free hostages because the situation dictates not a planned and prepared assault

EOD – Explosive Ordnance Disposal

Grizz it out – to tough it out, fight the pain

HAHO – High Altitude High Opening military free fall

Heli Exfil – an exfiltration performed using helicopters

Hellfire Missile – an air-to-ground missile first developed for anti-armour use, later developed for precision drone strikes against other target types, especially high-value targets

HESCO bastion – a wire mesh container or heavy duty fabric liner filled with sand that is used as a military fortification

HK416 – a gas-operated assault rifle

HLS – Helicopter Landing Site

IDF – Indirect Fire

IED – Improvised Explosive Device

ISAF – The International Security Assistance Force was a multinational military mission in Afghanistan from 2001 to 2014

JOC – Joint Operations Centre

JSOC – Joint Special Operations Command

JTAC – Joint Terminal Attack Controller

KAF – Kandahar Airfield (a NATO base in Afghanistan)

LO – Liaison Officer

LS – Landing Site

M4 – 5.56mm carbine weapon

MOD – Ministry of Defence

Mujahideen – mujahideen, or mujahidin, is the plural form of *mujahid*, an Arabic term that broadly refers to people who engage in jihad, interpreted in a jurisprudence of Islam as the fight on behalf of God, religion or the community

NATO – North Atlantic Treaty Organization

NCO – non-commissioned officer

NGO – non-governmental organisation

NVG – night-vision goggles

Number 10 – Reference to 10 Downing Street: The Prime Minister

OC – officer commanding a company

Op Herrick – the code name under which all British operations in the War in Afghanistan were conducted from 2002 to the end of combat operations in 2014

Pax – passengers or packages on a transport

RAF – Royal Air Force

ROE – Rules Of Engagement

RSM – Regimental Sergeant Major

SAS – Special Air Service

SBS – Special Boat Service

SEALs – A naval branch of US Special Operations Forces

SIS – Secret Intelligence Service

Sitrep – Situation Report

SNCO – Senior Non-commissioned Officer

SOF – United States Special Operations Forces

SOP – Standard Operating Procedure

SSM – Squadron Sergeant Major

Taliban – a fundamentalist and nationalist militant political movement in Afghanistan

Two-ship – two Apache helicopters flying in support.

UKSF – United Kingdom Special Forces

USAF – United States Air Force

USSR – Union of Soviet Socialist Republics

WSO – Weapons System Operator